BALANCE

IS

B.S.

BALANCE IS B.S.

HOW TO HAVE A

work. life. *blend.*

TAMARA LOEHR

WILEY

Published by John Wiley & Sons, Inc., Hoboken, New Jersey.
Published simultaneously in Canada.

For general information on our other products and services or for technical support, please contact our Customer Care Department within the United States at (800) 762-2974, outside the United States at (317) 572-3993 or fax (317) 572-4002.

Wiley publishes in a variety of print and electronic formats and by print-on-demand. Some material included with standard print versions of this book may not be included in e-books or in print-on-demand. If this book refers to media such as a CD or DVD that is not included in the version you purchased, you may download this material at http://booksupport.wiley.com. For more information about Wiley products, visit www.wiley.com.

Library of Congress Cataloging-in-Publication Data is Available:
ISBN 978-1-119-55040-2 (Hardcover)
ISBN 978-1-119-55044-0 (ePDF)
ISBN 978-1-119-55045-7 (ePub)

Cover design and illustration: Zoltán Nemes

Printed in the United States of America

V10008439_022719

To Flori and my girls:

Thank you for your unconditional love.

I am infinitely grateful for our life,
the journey and adventures we share.

Contents

Work

Personal

PART III   Keep Blending for Life

Disclaimer

In this book, I'm going to talk about my husband and kids a lot, because that's the world I'm in (and because I love them). But I don't want this book to exclude you if you're not married, or don't have kids. For a while there I thought I was going to be a single mom—I was 29, in the middle of a divorce, and looking up sperm donors on the internet. So no judgment from me if you haven't followed the same path I have.

This book is for women who are doing big things in their careers, but also want to manage their personal lives well—whatever that means for you. So I've got chapters devoted to marriage and parenting, because this is what personal life looks like for a lot of us, and that's where gender roles mess with our heads the most. But I hope if you don't conform to the "husband and 2.5 kids" model, you still get a lot out of this book. If you're a woman who wants to rise without compromise, you're one of us.

Acknowledgments

The following people made valued personal contributions to the book: Daniel Bonney, Emily Diamond, Monte Heubsch, Gina Mollicone-Long, Sue-Ellen Watts, Aaron Zamykal and, of course, Florian Loehr.

Thank you to Jeff Hoffman, Keith Abraham, Paul Dunn and Michel Kripalani for your inspiring work and for permission to use your words.

An extra-special mention to:

Kamina: Thank you for taking my journal rants and vision for this book and making it come to life. Your talent is admirable and our new-found friendship is treasured. PS: You were a blender before we met!

Emily: Thank you for your life/business coaching and dear friendship. You've transformed so many lives, mine included, so thank you for taking the time to turn your invaluable methods into two-page exercises for this book. Continue your path of positively impacting the world!

K (Kylie): Thank you for showing me what unconditional friendship looks like. You lift me up, make me laugh, never judge, and lead with such a big heart. Blessed to call you bestie.

Florian: Thank you for empowering me, supporting me, and being my rock and the best role model to our children: shared values, constantly evolving, creating memories, and being adventurous.

PART I

Balance Is Bullshit

CHAPTER 1

Rising without Compromising

I met Florian when I was 31.

At 31, I had a plan. I'd grown my marketing agency to be one of the top agencies in Australia. I'd been working as a singer/songwriter for 15 years and had a couple of hit singles and toured Japan. I'd been married at 22 and divorced at 30. Everybody thought I was crazy when we broke up, but I think the partner you're with should think you're the best thing in the world. He didn't. And I didn't want to settle any more.

My plan was to wait until I was 35 and then become a single mother. My best friend and I had looked up sperm donors on the internet. It wasn't that I didn't want to get married again, it was just that I didn't want to compromise. And growing up in a mining town, I had certain perceptions about what marriage was: it seemed like everyone I went to school with got married, got pregnant, and had no inspiration to leave town. So I'd made a different plan for my life.

Florian wasn't in the plan.

I was 31, and I'd decided to retire from the music industry. My last gig was in Morocco, at a festival in Essaouira. Then I was due to fly to Japan, but there was a typhoon in Japan so I got stuck in London for a night. I really didn't care for London (mainly due to the weather), but I was put up in this beautiful hotel. Florian was working at the front desk.

Florian's a real romantic. He'd just gotten back from his grandparents' 60th-anniversary party and he was working behind the desk at this hotel. He saw me walk in and thought "holy shit" and basically pushed people out of the way so he could serve me.

I handed my passport across the desk and he saw that our birthdays were one week apart. He took it as a sign.

I said to my travel companion, "I am going to give him my number because he's cute and we're having 'butterfly' moments," and she said, "he's gay! Man, you can't even pick it any more!"

I gladly proved her wrong.

We started talking every day. He'd fly over and meet me and we'd rendezvous in wineries. I was scared to show him my businesses and my block of units, my real life. I had this stupid theory that successful women scare men away, so I tried to downplay it all.

When I met him, I didn't know he'd been raised by a working mother and a stay-at-home dad. I didn't know he had two sisters and admired strong women.

I didn't know that he'd see raising children as a job, not an afterthought, and it was a job he really wanted to do.

I didn't know that eight years later he'd be living with me and our two kids in our home in Australia. That I'd be taking him to business functions and getting used to men talking to him and ignoring me, assuming he was the entrepreneur and I was the trophy wife.

I didn't know he was perfect for me. I just gave him my email address and ran away.

****

So we did get married, and I didn't have to compromise. Instead, our family joined the ranks of statistics like these:

- A 2013 study found that in 40% percent of American households with children under 18, the primary breadwinner was a woman. Of these, 37% were households where the woman was married and earned more than her husband.[1]
- In Australia in 2017, 52% of all women, and 57% of those who lived with a partner and no kids, identified themselves as the main earner. In couples with kids, 25% of them were supported by a female breadwinner.[2]

There's been a huge shift in female earning, and it's happened really quickly. In the 1960s, for example, only 6% of US households had female breadwinners, as opposed to roughly 40% now.[3] In Australia, women's real annual earnings have risen by 82% in the past 30 years, compared to only 16% for men, because women started from a much lower baseline.[4] Women are not only earning more in general, but some of us are starting to earn more than our male partners. A lot more.

And those stats keep rising.

All of which is incredible for women. Yes, we have a long way to go with closing the pay gap. Yes, in general, there are still far fewer women than men in executive and board positions, across any country or sector you take a look at. But it's a changing game, and it's changing quickly. Female earning is on the rise. Rates of female breadwinners are on the rise. Females are rising through company ranks and taking on more responsibility, more prestigious titles, and more lucrative salaries.

This is not only incredible for women, individually and globally—it's really fucking good for business.

> If you replaced all of the prime ministers and presidents of all the countries in the world with women, within a generation there'd be no war. Women's conflict resolution isn't to punch each other. Women being expected to behave like men in the workplace—therein lies the problem. If all we're doing is remaking women into the image of men, we're losing 90% of the value that they bring.
>
> —Monte Huebsch, "The Google Guru @ Aussieweb"

As more women have started showing up on boards around the world, people have started questioning the impact—for better or worse—of higher female involvement on the performance of the companies. And study after study has found that companies with more women among their C-level staff outperform companies that have few or no women in similar positions.

- A Catalyst study examined 353 companies that remained on the Fortune 500 list for four out of five years from 1996 to 2000. It found that **"companies with a higher representation of women in senior management positions financially outperform companies with proportionally fewer women at the top."**[5]
- CreditSuisse's 2014 CS Gender 3000 study, which mapped over 28,000 senior managers at over 3,000 companies worldwide, demonstrated that **"companies with higher female representation at the board level or in top management exhibit higher returns on equity, higher valuations and also higher payout ratios."**[6]

- A 2017 report by McKinsey assimilated 10 years of research into female participation in the workforce and concluded that **"closing—or even narrowing—the global gender gap in work would not only be equitable in the broadest sense but could have significant economic impact** ... as much as $12 trillion could be added to annual global GDP growth in 2025, or 11% to global 2025 GDP."[7]

These are just a few examples. I'm sure emerging data will continue to show that female participation is good for business, both at the level of individual companies and at the level of global economic development.

It's not really clear whether more women in a business make the company run "better," or whether "better" corporations tend to employ and appoint more women. It probably goes both ways and it doesn't really matter: the point is that gender diversity and good business go hand in hand. It's good for the world and good for us ambitious women. But all this goodness is giving rise to a problem that's really hard to talk about.

Across working households, women are working more *outside* the home, but they're not really working less *inside* the home.

In studies of couples where both the man and woman work full-time, the overwhelming finding is that the women do more housework on average than the men. Men are definitely doing more at home than they used to, but women still have a tendency to burden themselves with most of the household management.

This is before you factor in taking care of kids, which women also expect themselves to handle even when they're working full-time outside the home. What mother hasn't felt guilty when she has to go to work and leave her babies? That "mommy, don't go"—it breaks your heart. (This is twice as hard for single moms, who feel 100% responsible for their kids' emotional needs.)

And women always put their personal stuff last—self care, friendships, personal goals, fun—because nobody is hassling us or complaining if we don't get those things done.

We're lifting our expectations of ourselves in our careers, but we're not adjusting our expectations around our partnerships, parenting, and everything else we've got going on in our personal lives. We're compromising like crazy to try to "have it all" but we don't have all the things we really want.

We're all in pursuit of the elusive "work-life balance" and feeling guilty because it's impossible to get there. I'm here to tell you that the concept is faulty, not you. Balance is bullshit. There is a better way.

My dream is that this book will help you do these things:

- Shut down the myth that work-life balance is possible, or even something you want to pursue.
- Let go of guilt and blend your work and personal life in a way that doesn't burn you out.
- Stop being disappointed by plans and live according to your values instead.
- Learn how to have important conversations with key people in your life so that everyone's expectations are the same.
- Get your shit together and write a strategy for doing the things you actually want to do.

That's the journey we're going to go on together in this book.

It's important to get this right, because those stats are going to keep rising.

So let's rise with them. Let's call bullshit on the myths that keep us down, and create a community of women committed to rising without compromising.

NOTES

1. W. Wang, K. Parker, and P. Taylor, "Breadwinner Moms: Mothers Are the Sole or Primary Provider in Four-in-Ten Households with Children; Public Conflicted about the Growing Trend," Pew Research Center, May 29, 2013, http://www.pewsocialtrends.org/2013/05/29/breadwinner-moms/.
2. S. Richardson J. Healy, and M. Moskos, "From 'Gentle Invaders' to 'Breadwinners': Australian Women's Increasing Employment and Earnings Shares," Flinders University NILS Working Paper Series No. 210, September 2014, http://www.flinders.edu.au/sabs/nils-files/publications/working-papers/Breadwinner%20Women.pdf.
3. Wang et al. 2013, "Breadwinner Moms."
4. Richardson et al, 2014, "From 'Gentle Invaders' to 'Breadwinners.'"
5. Catalyst 2004, "The Bottom Line: Connecting Corporate Performance and Gender Diversity," Catalyst, January 15, 2004, http://www.catalyst.org/system/files/The_Bottom_Line_Connecting_Corporate_Performance_and_Gender_Diversity.pdf.

6. M. Curtis, C. Schmid, and M. Struber, "Gender Diversity and Corporate Performance," CreditSuisse Research Institute, accessed June 6, 2018, https://www
.calstrs.com/sites/main/files/file-attachments/csri_gender_diversity_and_corporate_
performance.pdf.
7. J. Woetzel et al., "The Power of Parity: How Advancing Women's Equality Can
Add $12 Trillion to Global Growth," McKinsey Global Institute, September 2015,
https://www.mckinsey.com/~/media/McKinsey/Featured-Insights/Employment-and-
Growth/How-advancing-womens-equality-can-add-12-trillion-to-global-growth/MGI-
Power-of-parity_Full-report_September-2015.ashx.

CHAPTER 2

The Myths That Keep Us Down

> In the earlier stages of feminism, women were told they could not be whatever it was they wanted to be. After women became those things anyway, then society said, "All right, you're now a lawyer or a mechanic or an astronaut—but that's only okay if you continue to do the work you did before—if you take care of the children, cook three meals a day, and are multiorgasmic until dawn."[1]
>
> —Gloria Steinem, journalist and activist

Before we can rise above, we've got to tear some things down. There are myths we believe without even realizing that we can opt out and live a different way. There are scripts that play in our heads and tell us that if we just tried a little bit harder, we'd get it all right.

"Women can have it all!"

"I can't have it all."

"If I'm successful at work, I must be failing at home."

"I'm missing out."

"My husband is missing out."

"I just need a work-life balance."

The idea that you can find the perfect balance is the biggest myth of all. Even when you find a rhythm that works for you, you won't get it right all the time. I don't.

But you *can* shut down the voice in your head that says you have to do things a certain way, provide a certain amount of time to your family, and be a certain type of person at work in order to have a good "work-life balance." I think the balance we're chasing is bullshit, actually. But we'll get to that after we've talked about some of the biggest myths that get in our way.

THE MYTH OF WHAT MAKES US WORTHY, ACCORDING TO OUR GENDER

Sensitivity around traditional gender roles seems highest in couples where the woman not only has a career outside the home, but earns more than her husband does. One study on gender identity and income came to this *unbelievable* conclusion about couples where the wife is the higher earner: "When the wife brings in more money, couples often revert to more stereotypical sex roles; in such cases, wives typically take on a larger share of household work and child care."[2]

A *larger* share!? Who's got time for that?

The economists justified it like this: "Our analysis of the time use data suggests that gender identity considerations may lead a woman who seems threatening to her husband because she earns more than he does to engage in a larger share of home production activities, particularly household chores."[3]

In her feminist memoir *The Fictional Woman*, Tara Moss elaborates:

> One posited explanation for this seemingly illogical phe-nomenon is that the division of housework and the effort put into the performance of the traditional good wife role is a conscious or unconscious strategy by one or both spouses to avoid criticism for the woman's choice to have a high-powered career, and the fact that the man's choice, or circumstance, means he does not occupy that expected breadwinner role ... basically, she has to be seen as not neglecting her wifely duties (See, I'm still a good wife! I'm still a good mother!) and he doesn't want to risk further deviating from gender expectations by taking on "feminine" duties.[4]

So the woman in this scenario is doing more work at home to *make up for* the fact that she's contributing more money to the household than her husband. Like a huge apology. What the fuck.

We're culturally conditioned to value men according to how much money they make, so if we make more money than our husband, we feel like we're taking away his worth. And we feel so guilty about it that we try to act super-feminine—by doing extra work at home, because that's apparently what makes us a woman—to build up his masculinity and reassure him that his role hasn't disappeared.

Not only that, but we've been programmed to value *ourselves* according to how much our husband makes, instead of how much we make. So as our capacity to outearn our husband goes up, our feeling of worthiness goes down.

> *It wasn't all that long ago that many women were valued solely by the size of the money their fathers could contribute as a dowry, or by the size of their husband's wealth and the value it brought to their families.... If we married "down," we were literally worth less (or "worthless") in the eyes of our culture—shunned, chastised, devalued. If we married "up," however, we were worth more, having served our appropriate role as currency in the negotiations of men seeking to build wealth and power.*[5]
> —Elizabeth Cronise McLaughlin, founder of the Gaia Leadership Project for Women's Leadership

We're kicking goals and making amazing shit happen in our businesses. We're providing for our families, maybe even earning more than our husbands. But we don't relax and enjoy those wins—we feel ashamed of them.

The craziest part in all of this is that most of us haven't even checked in to see if our husbands feel the way we think they do. Nobody's actually asking us to earn less or do more at home. We're assuming that's what he wants and putting it all on ourselves, and we haven't even had the conversation. (We'll dig deeper into that in Chapters 13 and 14.)

THE MYTH OF "HAVING IT ALL"

We're told that women can have it all. So we put pressure on ourselves to achieve that. Now that we've managed to break into the business arena, we don't want to mess it up by admitting that we have to make some compromises. So we tell ourselves it's possible to be 100% invested and kicking goals at work and 100% present at home as a wife and mother. *It must be possible! We're supposed to have it all!*

The reality is, 100% investment in every area all the time isn't possible. It's never going to happen, and when we try it and fail we just feel guilty. So the script in our heads is telling us that we can't *really* have it all, even while we keep pretending to try. It's a recipe for more guilt, more shame, more overwhelm. Instead of celebrating our high-powered, high-earning careers, we're worried that our husbands feel threatened and our kids feel neglected. Instead of enjoying our marriages, our children, and our social lives, we're half-thinking about work all the time.

But I think women *can* have it all. I feel like I do.

It's just that "having it all" might look different than the picture we've had in our heads. It might look like taking your husband with you on your business trips and enjoying kid-free time on the plane. It might be encouraging your employees' personal goals outside of work, to build a culture of reminding people in your company (including yourself) that they're human. You might choose to employ people you're friends with so that you can spend more time with them day-to-day.

You might just have to be more choosy about where you invest and when, and make the decision to get over anxiety about missing out on the things you're not investing in right now. I like to say you can have it all, but you can't always have it all at the same time. I can "have it all" in terms of having everything I want right now, today, but that doesn't mean I want everything all at once.

THE MYTH OF "WORK-LIFE BALANCE"

The concept of "work-life balance" carries a whole mess of problems.

Firstly, "balance" is usually talked about as a female problem, not a male one. When's the last time you heard a man talk about "work-life balance" or "having it all"? It feels normal for a man to work *and* have children *and* a social life; nobody praises that guy for managing to "have it all." So let's shut down this bullshit about women needing some type of special balancing skills (that men apparently don't) to achieve a basic level of satisfaction both personally and professionally.

Secondly, the term *work-life balance* is designed to make us feel shitty about work. It implies that "work" isn't really part of "life," but just a thing you have to get through to enjoy the rest of your time. Excuse me, but I actually love my work. I love my kids, my husband, and my home, too, but it's not one over the other. I'm not trying to get the "balance" right so that I can spend as little time as possible working.

We're told what work-life balance is supposed to look like: We're meant to switch our phones off during family time, take regular vacations, and refuse to look at work emails after hours. But what's waiting for us when we get back? The emails and task list don't go away, so the work piles up. The thought of this gives me anxiety!

The problem is that most entrepreneurs aren't made for that kind of balance. We want to do everything well, all the time. And our business identity is so closely tied to our personal identity that it isn't easy for us to just switch off work mode. Work is part of who we are when we're flourishing. Work is part of life; they're not opposites.

If we try to compartmentalize our time, we just end up feeling guilty *all* the time. When we're at work, we feel guilty for our families. And when we're at home, we feel the pull to be involved with what's going on at work. The truth is, we love them both. And we try to make them incompatible with each other when they shouldn't be.

I'm calling it: It's bullshit. **Balance is bullshit.**

So what are you going to do about it?

NOTES

1. G. Steinem, "Gloria Stenem's Commencement Speech to the Class of 1988," *Wellesley College Commencement Archives*, May 27, 1988, https://www.wellesley.edu/events/commencement/archives/1988Commencement/commencementaddress.
2. C. Rampell, "U.S. Women on the Rise as Family Breadwinner," *New York Times*, May 29, 2013, https://www.nytimes.com/2013/05/30/business/economy/women-as-family-breadwinner-on-the-rise-study-says.html.

3. This and the previous note are referencing M. Bertrand, J. Pan, and E. Kamenica, "Gender Identity and Relative Income within Households," *The Quarterly Journal of Economics* 130, no. 2 (2013): 571–614, http://www.nber.org/papers/w19023>.

4. T. Moss, *The Fictional Woman* (HarperCollins Publishers, 2014), 143.

5. E. Cronise McLaughlin, "I Used to Be Ashamed of Making More Money Than My Husband. Not Anymore," *Huffington Post*, January 27, 2015, https://www.huffingtonpost.com/40-percent-and-rising/i-make-more-money-than-my-husband_b_6467552.html.

CHAPTER 3

Balance Is Bullshit: Blend Instead

Whenever I do a speaking gig somewhere nice, I take my family and we have a mini holiday.

At the end the MC always says, "I'm sure everybody in the audience has lots of questions, so are you happy for people to come up to you?" And I unapologetically tell them where to find me if they want more: "No problem, but I'm here with my family so if you want to speak to me I'll be in the pool playing with them. You're welcome to come up and ask me anything."

And they do. And I answer what I can, to these guys in suits hanging around the pool, getting splashed by my kids. I'm pretty sure I'm the only entrepreneur at the conference giving business advice in her bikini.

****

That old idiom that you should keep business and pleasure separate is dead.

You're human. Your colleagues know that. If I weren't friends with the people I work with I'd never have any friends. (My friends joke that the best way to get me to spend time with them is to go into business with me.)

It doesn't make you unprofessional to admit that you're answering a work call from home, or during the school pickup run. You don't have to find a quiet corner and pretend to be in an office when somebody "important" calls. And you don't have to feel guilty for taking that call on the weekend. You love your work, don't you? Sometimes it needs you, just like your family does.

In the same way, you need to give yourself permission to have some availability for personal things during work hours. There's plenty of evidence that allowing people to be more "human" at work actually benefits the organization and increases productivity, not the other way around. So cut yourself some slack. If you duck out early some days to do the school run, you're going to impact your day's work about 5% and improve your family-related guilt about 1,000%. So go for it.

It's just not realistic to manage your personal life and run your business or career well without this flexibility.

So what's my answer to work-life balance? My friends and I call it **blending**.

We're all familiar with the picture of "work-life balance": It's a woman standing with her arms stretched out on either side, work stuff balanced in one hand and personal stuff in the other. Or a set of scales with career on one side and personal on the other. Your job is to get both sides to balance each other out.

What if you just threw away the scales and chucked all of it in a blender? And depending on your priorities and what you feel like at any moment, you're allowed to blend in anything you want.

Depending on how I feel today, maybe I'll blend afternoon drinks with my friends with a discussion about the business projects we're across together. Or I'll blend the school run with a work call (and if I call you from the car with my kids, they'll be saying hi to you on speakerphone).

It's important to respect people's time and ask for permission, but their having to put up with a bit of background noise and a quick hello from the kids often outweighs them having to wait until tomorrow for an answer or some direction.

It's all about giving attention to what's important right now, without worrying about whether you're on the clock or not. It's about managing your commitments so that everything you want to do gets done, without forcing yourself to conform to "work time" and "personal time."

In Part II of this book, we're going to get into every area of your life and talk about how you can blend across them all, so that you're always giving your energy to what's most important.

Here are some examples of what makes it work for me:

- My executive assistant knows *everything* about me. Her job description is totally blended, personal and professional: She's across everything. Having an assistant who's on top of everything in my life is the only way I can make it work.

- In my organizations, we don't have any meetings before 9:15 a.m. or in the evenings. We do daytime meetings and lunches only, so that people can drop their kids at school and be home with them at night (or I have the team around for a barbecue and we talk business while the kids are playing). On the other hand, if a staff member is at their child's soccer game and they get a work call, I'd encourage them to take it if they can. My staff know it's fine to say, "I'm at the kids' soccer game. I can talk for five minutes."
- If I have to go away for two weeks or more for work, the family comes with me. When I do go away by myself, I extend the break for half a day per every day that I'm away, and spend some time with the family at the beach or somewhere away from home once I return. I go back to work with my batteries recharged.

Obviously your blending choices aren't going to be the same as mine, because your life isn't set up exactly the same as mine. You might be reading this and thinking "good for you, but I couldn't do those things." That's fine—what *could* you do?

Take a second now and imagine how blending might work for you. What kind of freedom could you create if you let go of the idea of work-life balance and started blending instead?

- What would change if you stopped apologizing to your husband and kids for giving attention to your work, and instead showed them how much you love it? Or invited them to be involved?
- How empowered would you feel if you started setting boundaries unapologetically around work, and managed your time according to what you *know* serves your productivity best, instead of what makes you look like a hard worker?
- How free would you be if you stopped switching between different versions of yourself and started being the same person all the time—whether you were with your family, on a date, drinking with your girlfriends, or talking to your colleagues?

All of that is possible. You just have to know what you value most, promise not to compromise, and live unapologetically in line with what's most important to you. It isn't always easy—it's bloody hard sometimes—but that's why I'm writing this book. I'm inviting you to become part of a new wave of women, a community committed to rising without compromising.

I read this great story about Sallie Krawcheck (who was at the time the CEO of Citigroup's Smith Barney division), told by her colleague Anne Greenwood:

> *About six months into Krawcheck's tenure, the company announced an all-office conference call. "It's very unusual to have all 600 managers from all offices call in—not unheard-of, but you don't do it that often, because a Wall Street firm doesn't want to freeze everybody."*
>
> *The call begins and Krawcheck starts talking. Suddenly, she interrupts herself, Greenwood recalls. "She says, 'Everyone please bear with me, I have to put the call on hold.' We're thinking, okay, the head of the Federal Reserve Board must be calling. Something huge has happened in the world economic space."*
>
> *Ninety seconds later, Krawcheck comes back on the line. Greenwood remembers what she said next as if it happened yesterday. "She says, 'I'm so sorry, you guys, that was my daughter and I promised her that she could always reach me. I made a deal with her that if I take this big job, no matter where I am, what I'm doing or who I'm with, I will take your call. The funny thing is, she couldn't find the pink nail polish. I'm the only one who knows it's in the upstairs bathroom.'"*
>
> *"Immediately there was buzz among the few women in elite positions around the firm," says Greenwood. "I couldn't believe she was so honest about what had happened. Never in a million years would I have told a male workforce that my daughter couldn't find the pink nail polish."[1]*

If one of the most senior women on Wall Street can do it, so can you.

NOTE

1. Anne Greenwood quoted by A. Jones, "Sallie Krawcheck Wants to Take Women to the Top of Business," *Newsweek*, December 23, 2014, http://www.newsweek.com/2015/01/02/sallie-krawcheck-wants-take-women-top-business-294332.html.

PART II

A Workbook for Rising Women

CHAPTER 4

"Moving Up" versus Rising

How to use this book to lift up every area of your life

People are always talking about "moving up in the world."

"Climbing the corporate ladder."

"I upgraded my man."

No, no, no. I don't want us to "move" up. I want us to *rise up*.

Rising up doesn't actually mean achieving success in a traditional sense. It means rising above: Rising above stereotypes. Rising above learned behavior. Rising up the level of your self-worth. Rising up to become a version of yourself that's aligned with your values. Making no compromises.

Rising is about having more choices and more clarity. Having higher personal values that complement each other and don't get compromised. It means having the relationships I want, and making them amazing. Having the type of vocation that I want, the kind of physical life that I want, expressing my emotions the way I want to. Not settling, not juggling, not climbing.

Once you've got the foundations right and adopted a "rising" attitude, the other successes will follow:

- You'll get clarity in your business and know which activities to invest your energy in to get the best results.
- You'll feel less mommy-guilt because you'll set your life up to spend time on what's most important, and unapologetically ditch the shit that doesn't matter.

- You'll know how to communicate constructively with your partner about how to run your lives together.
- You'll surround yourself with people who are a good fit for you and instinctively create a culture in your workplace that fosters positivity, productivity, and flow.

So how do we make it happen?

If you want to rise, there are some rules. The type of woman I'm talking about—the type of woman I try to be, and I want you to be—has a few key qualities:

- She's flexible.
- She's strong.
- She's responsive.

And she knows a few things about herself:

- She knows her *value* and she knows her *values*.
- She knows how to navigate life according to her values, not her plans.
- She knows what to do when her values are in conflict.
- And she knows how to apply this in all the key areas of her life.

In other words, she's a pretty emotionally sophisticated woman.

Above all, your values need to be nonnegotiable. Once you know yourself well enough to know what your values are, you can learn how to hold them high in every area of life. The rest will fall into place if you stop fighting the things that are most important to you.

This all started to come together for me after I met my coach, Emily Diamond, who provided the exercises for this book.

It was around 2008 or 2009 that I decided I needed a coach. I'd been studying the traits of effective entrepreneurs and one thing they all said was that it was crucial to have a business coach. So I asked my lecturer at the National College of Business if he knew somebody who could coach me. I wanted the coaching to be about more than just business; I wanted somebody who could give me life coaching as well. The first person he referred me to didn't work out, so then he referred me to Emily. We clicked right away; like most good things in my life, it was a gut instinct thing for me. Emily reckons she got a sign, which is crazy because Florian got a sign when he first met me too. That's two significant people in my life.

The way Emily tells it, she was sent in to salvage the relationship after my meeting with that first coach didn't go well. She walked into my office to meet me for the first time and I had one of those day-to-a-page desk calendars with a quote on each page. I had it open to her birthday. And the quote was something about effectiveness of communication, which she loves. That was her sign.

So we started working together. My career has changed so much in the time I've known her, but she's always brought the conversation back to values. It's always been about how to be a better leader, a better partner, a better human. And if I say something that contradicts my values she'll flag it.

Fundamental to how I've managed to stay focused, sane, and honest is having someone who calls me on my values throughout the journey. Throughout our eight years together there have been a lot of tools that I've used across all areas, and now my team is using them. These are techniques and exercises that have enriched my life and given me clarity. I want to share them with you, so they're going to form the basis of this workbook.

In order to help you sort through shit and start blending, the workbook is going to guide you to assess your values based on how you operate in every area of life. Then you can see which areas aren't fulfilling you according to your values, which areas are in conflict, and how to bring it all into alignment.

CATEGORIZE, DON'T COMPARTMENTALIZE

I know what you're thinking: *She just spent three chapters telling me to blend my life together and stop compartmentalizing. Now she's saying I have to categorize everything under different areas of my life and consider each area separately!? Is she full of shit with this whole blending thing?*

No, I'm not! (At least, not about this.)

Think of these categories as tools for navigation, not a call to compartmentalize. "Life" is a huge category; we need to break it down for the purpose of working through it and identifying the areas that need the most attention. Once you adopt the rising attitude, you'll naturally start to integrate all the areas of your life and blend them together.

Emily has a neuroscience background, so I trust her when she says that compartmentalizing is dangerous, but blending is good for your brain.

Call in the Coach: Emily on Multitasking versus Blending

When we say blending, we're not talking about multitasking. We all know that multitasking impairs your performance.

Being a different version of yourself to everybody is actually a more sophisticated version of multitasking. So when we're talking about blending, we're talking about the opposite of multitasking. It's blending and integration instead of multitasking and compartmentalization.

Some people love to sit down and carve up their diary: Work is only during these hours, family is that time, sports go here, me time is there. This sounds good in theory, but you start to run into problems—for example, if you have to go to a specialist appointment during work hours, what happens then?

What happens is that stress arises. Even if you're passionate about your work, or love your family, the inability to carve up your time the way you've planned—the conflict of reality with the plans you've laid—causes stress.

When you're stressed, there's no blood in your frontal lobe. That's where your creativity, your resources, and your genius lie. It's also where you get your ability to plan well and make high-quality decisions.

It's simple: When people are stressed, they make poor decisions. (We've all seen what we buy online when we're tired, or who we've gone home with when we're upset.) Life is a product of the decisions you make. If you're making decisions while being impaired by stress all the time, your life is not going to be how you want it to be.

> *Different areas of your life are always going to be competing for your attention; if you try to compartmentalize all the time you're kidding yourself. When you're integrated you'll have less stress. Suddenly you'll find you have the life you want and you're getting to enjoy it, too.*
>
> *We're all about paving the way for less stress and better decisions. This whole book is about integrating every area of your life so that you can do that. We want to give your frontal lobe some blood back so it can do some good shit!*

I've divided my life into areas that make sense to me, but at the end of the day I want you to approach your life as a whole thing, knowing where to emphasize your energy and where to pull back day to day depending on your priorities.

This is how we're going to approach it for the purposes of this book.

1. Self

This covers your spiritual, emotional, intellectual, and physical well-being. It's about knowing yourself, doing things that fill your soul, and continuing to grow as a person.

2. Work

This is about your vocation—whatever your main daily occupation is, whether you have a job, run a business, or pursue a different kind of endeavor. It also covers how you handle the responsibility of being a breadwinner and prioritize what to do with your money.

3. Personal

This is how you operate outside of the work sphere: in your romantic partnership (if you have one), your immediate family unit, your friends, and close community. It's also about the way you contribute to society by giving back.

Of course, because we're talking about blending, the different areas of your life are going to overlap. Your closest friends might come from your business community. Your sense of self might be fulfilled by work achievements or by spending time with your family. As you work through the different areas, you'll notice how they impact each other and how you can invest time and energy into activities that will feed multiple areas. That's the beauty of blending.

HOW TO USE THIS BOOK

Before you can start doing the work, you need to lay some foundations. That's what the next three chapters are for. They'll set you up with the concepts that you need before you can get into the workbook.

From there, you can go to any section of the book that you like and do the exercises that relate to you. (There's an index of exercises at the back of the book for reference.) Of course, I recommend that you give consideration to all the bits of life in due course. And if you're not sure where to start, just start at the beginning and work through it all.

You can read this book however works best for you—on the plane, on your commute, in bed at night—but when you see a coaching exercise, stop and consider it, or come back to it later. These DIY sessions are best done with a pen and paper. They won't take long, but it's worth setting aside some time and energy to give them your full attention.

If your reading time is limited, just go slowly and thoroughly. If you give yourself a year to work through the whole thing with proper attention, you could spend four weeks working on the area covered in each chapter and have some vacation time left over.

Once you've worked through the exercises in every chapter, you'll have a beautiful bucket list filled with items that cover the whole spectrum of your life and what's important to you. You'll be equipped to create a road map for doing what you want, how you want to do it, when you want to—which is what we'll cover in the final section of this book. And you should find yourself starting to blend without thinking twice, and without compromising on anything important.

If you're burning to address a particular problem or conflict in your life right away, start there. Feel free to jump into whichever area is most important to you right now, or is giving you the least amount of workability.

But don't go there until you've read the next three chapters!

CHAPTER **5**

V Squared

How to know your values and know your value

**Call in the Coach: Emily on
Exhaustion versus Integration**

*Consider the sources of exhaustion for a modern woman: trying
to be everything to everyone, trying to be everywhere all the time,
trying to be on top of everything, trying to remember everything,
trying to do everything, taking responsibility for everything, and
then trying to be a different person in every environment. So I've
got to be my work version, my house version, my mommy version.*

*The ultimate test is this: If you can be the same person, in
the same mode, with the same sense of humor, telling the same
jokes with your parents, with your best friend, at work, with your
children (maybe just with more appropriate language)—you are
integrated. Being fragmented is the source of the exhaustion.*

I travel a lot. Not because I have to, but because I like travel. I get
my best ideas on planes. But I don't fucking fly coach, because that's not
properly valuing my time. I lose a day either side, and I want to be present
with my family when I get back.

I don't do TV. I don't cook or clean. I don't do acquaintances. I don't
have an abundance of friends. I'm happy not to return phone calls from
all the ladies at school who invite me to lunch. I don't care what people

think any more because otherwise I'm just filling your diary and don't do anything for myself. You have a choice: care about what other people think or care about what you think. If it doesn't suit your values and it doesn't excite you, just don't do it.

That sounds really self-serving, but it took me a long time to get to that point—because I *always* care what people think.

I was always a victim of tall poppy syndrome. That's an Australian expression. The saying goes that in our culture, tall poppies get cut down. If you stand out too much above the crowd—if you're too different, too successful, achieve too much—people don't like it. Our natural desire is to cut down the tallest poppies to the same size as all the other flowers in the field.

But I can't help sticking out. I've had to get comfortable with the fact that I don't want to make the same choices as everybody else when it comes to how I do business or what type of mother I am. I can't let myself care if other people don't like it.

I know how to make these calls because I know what I value most. If I didn't know my values, I wouldn't feel as confident about how to spend my time and where to put my energy. I'd feel guilty about all the things I don't do, because I'd be worried about what I'm "supposed" to do instead of worrying about what actually matters to me. But I'm happy with my choices because I know they align with the things that are core to who I am.

KNOW YOUR VALUE

Before you can apply your *values*, you need to recognize your *value*.

I think knowing your value is about self-worth and self-respect. It's not necessarily about believing in your worth or value in a monetary sense (although it could be in certain situations, like if you're negotiating a job or a deal). It's more about understanding your own strengths and responding when you're expected to be part of something that doesn't play to those. If you know your own worth, if you value your time and energy and skills properly, you'll be able to say no with confidence. Knowing your value gives you the courage to walk away from things that aren't right.

It also gives you the courage to step up. You'll rise to a challenge, because you have a realistic sense of your own talent that tells you that you should be capable. You'll be brave enough to show up emotionally in your relationships and be vulnerable, because you recognize the value that you bring to those people and interactions.

When you recognize the things about yourself that are most valuable, you make room to express them and say no to other things that don't maximize your value. You know what's valuable to your family and your business, so you focus on doing those things. You let other people fill in the gaps where you don't bring as much to the table. Knowing your value helps you prioritize and make the best use of your time in all areas. Is the best use of my time cooking, or spending time with the kids? Is it being a control freak at work or empowering others and sticking to what I do best?

Knowing your value means having a realistic understanding of what you have to offer in every area of your life, and how best to offer it.

NAVIGATE LIFE ACCORDING TO YOUR VALUES, NOT YOUR PLANS

Women love plans. Don't we?

I mean, we write fucking birth plans—as if that's something you can plan for. You might think you're totally dedicated to a drug-free birth, but when you're in the moment and you're in actual pain, you might want to change the plan. Having a birth plan is like the ultimate example of the way we like to plan for things we can't control.

The same goes for life. You plan and you plan and then shit hits the fan, you're screaming in pain and you want to change the plan. Or the situation is out of your control and your plan goes out the window.

Having a birth plan, a life plan, any kind of set-in-stone plan—that's a great way to set yourself up for disappointment.

That's why I talk about values over plans. It's fine to have a plan. But when the plan turns to shit you need to know how to roll with the changes. You want to be weaving your way through life, being challenged, navigating those challenges and changes with confidence. The best way to operate is to know your values so you can make good decisions in the moment.

It's futile to write a life plan that lists everything you think you'll want and need for the rest of your life. You'll usually end up being wrong, pursuing a list of achievements you set up when you didn't know what you didn't know. At different phases of your life your priorities will shift, but your values will always be there to guide you.

What you prioritize in your twenties will be different from what you prioritize in your thirties and forties. In my twenties, my big thing was that I had to be asset-rich, which to me meant owning property. That was the only tangible investment I understood. Then I got into my thirties and realized, *wow—the best thing I can invest in is actually myself. Shit, that pays a way bigger dividend!* So my perspective on assets and investment shifted.

In my twenties, my work life was just about imagining what it would be like to have a sustainable business. In my thirties, when I'd achieved that, it was about getting the business to serve me: finding ways to have flexibility and take more time off, especially because I had small children. I don't know what I'll want in my forties. "Making it all less complex" seems to be the theme so far.

My preferences around where I want to live have shifted. In my twenties the dream was a penthouse within walking distance to live music and bars. In my thirties it was the family home with the white picket fence and open space for my kids. In both cases it was about having a home that honored the things that were most important to me during that phase of my life.

I'm not fixated on being able to draw an exact picture of what my life will look like in the future; I just know that I will always live where it serves me best. I will always invest in things that I'm passionate about. And I probably won't follow the path that's easy and comfortable; I'll always be more likely to do what excites and challenges me.

HOW TO DEFINE YOUR VALUES

If you do an honest audit of how you spend your time, who you spend it with, how you fill your space, and where your money goes, it will reveal what you value most.

If you do the values audit and feel like you're spending your time, money, and energy on things that aren't fulfilling to you, this reveals something important about your values. It shows that you've got an underlying value that's overriding other values. Something bigger might be edging out the things that you really wish you could honor.

For example, your underlying value might be about wanting to fit in socially—you want to conform to what other people are doing and fulfill their expectations, so that drives your choices, even if it means choosing things you don't truly want. Or maybe you're temporarily ignoring one value in pursuit of another (for example, compromising on your family life because you're chasing financial security). If you have values in some areas that are in conflict with values in other areas, one or the other will get squashed.

When I do a values audit of my work life, it reminds me that I really value personal growth. When I spend time in my businesses, I want it to be spent around people who think differently than me. I like working with people who intimidate me a little bit with their intelligence. I like to be the little fish, and I keep changing ponds.

But I've already mentioned that I value asset-building as well. The way I approach business is really annoying from an asset point of view, because if I stayed longer in each company I'd still be there when it grew really big. But I like working in startups. I know that asset-based wealth is a really good idea, but I'm not going to accumulate it at the expense of growing and challenging myself.

(Plus, I'd rather work with good people than rich people. I've earned the right to not put up with dickheads. That's a better reward than a fancy car.)

So I've got a values conflict that I have to negotiate all the time when I make business decisions: Often what's best in terms of building an asset isn't the best in terms of me continuing to grow, not going insane from boredom and not having to work with dickheads.

It's okay to have values that work against each other, as long as you're aware of it and make intentional choices. We'll talk about how to handle conflicting values later.

For now, we're going to start with a basic exercise to audit your values. You can do this broadly across your whole life, or you can revisit it and do it in a focused way for each area of your life.

Coaching Exercise: Values Audit

WITH EMILY

Babe, build the life that fulfills you.

A fulfilled and integrated life is one where you make your decisions from what matters to you.

What matters to us are called our *values*.

If you want to discover your values, the answers are in front of you!

Often we think our values are X and really they are Y.

The process of discovering your values has three steps:

1. *Values brain dump.* This is the longest part of the exercise, but it's the foundation for the rest.
2. *Values themes.* This helps you identify repetitions and common threads to determine your values.
3. *Values hierarchy.* This is where you figure out which values take priority over others.

VALUES BRAIN DUMP

The first step uncovers your values across different areas of your life by examining: how you use your time, who you interact with most, what you fill your space with and how you spend your money.

For each area, start by asking yourself the basic question —for example, How do I spend my time?

Then ask yourself: Why? For what purpose?

Keep asking why until you realize the value that's driving you.

Here are some examples:

Q. How do I spend my time?

A. At work.

Q. Why?

A. For money.

Q. For what purpose?
A. To feel in control. So I can do what I like.
Q. Why?
A. Because that makes me feel like I have freedom.

Can you tell what the value is? You guessed it: *freedom*.

Q. How do I spend my money?
A. I spend a high proportion on rent.
Q. Why?
A. Because I like living in the city center.
Q. For what purpose?
A. To be close to culture and friends.
Q. Why?
A. To feel connected. I need connection to feel like myself.

So the value is *connection*.

Q. Who do I spend my time with?
A. Lots of time with extended family.
Q. Why?
A. Because those relationships are the most important to me.
Q. Why?
A. Because blood is thicker than water.
Q. Why?
A. Because I experience who I am through family. It's my legacy, my sense of self, where I belong.

You might name this value *belonging*.
Values are abstract, emotional, and not complicated. They are usually single words that carry a bucketload of emotion for you. As soon as it appears on the paper you will know!

(Continued)

(Continued)

HOT TIP: If you hit a "blank spot" in this exercise, repeat the question until your brain pops out an answer. Please do not go deep into analysis paralysis with this one. If it doesn't pop out, come back to that one later.

1. My Time

Think through a typical week. It might help to look at your calendar or day planner. Expect at least three answers for this one.

Where do you spend the biggest percentage of your time?

What activities are you doing, and what's the purpose of doing them?

How do I spend my time?

Time #1

Why?

For what purpose?

For what purpose?

What does that represent?

Time #2

Why?

For what purpose?

For what purpose?

What does that represent?

Time #3

Why?

For what purpose?

For what purpose?

What does that represent?

Time #4

Why?

For what purpose?

For what purpose?

What does that represent?

2. My People

Name the people you spend most of your time with. These may be individuals or groups.

What's the commonality that brings you together?

Who do I spend my time with?

People #1

Why?

For what purpose?

For what purpose?

What does that represent?

People #2

Why?

For what purpose?

For what purpose?

What does that represent?

People #3

Why?

For what purpose?

For what purpose?

What does that represent?

(Continued)

(*Continued*)

People #4

Why?

For what purpose?

For what purpose?

What does that represent?

3. My Space

How do you fill your space and what types of objects take pride of place in your home? Comfortable furnishings? Family photos? Recipe books? Plants? Figure out the ones that feature most prominently.

What do I fill my space with?

Space #1

Why?

For what purpose?

For what purpose?

What does that represent?

Space #2

Why?

For what purpose?

For what purpose?

What does that represent?

Space #3

Why?

For what purpose?

For what purpose?

What does that represent?

Space #4

Why?

For what purpose?

For what purpose?

What does that represent?

4. My Money

What do I spend my money on? What do I buy without thinking about it? What do I allocate budget to that I don't question? Do I organize my money? Do I track my spending? Do I plan my money?

My Money: Spending #1

Why?

For what purpose?

For what purpose?

What does that represent?

My Money: Spending #2

Why?

For what purpose?

For what purpose?

What does that represent?

My Money: Spending #3

Why?

For what purpose?

For what purpose?

What does that represent?

(Continued)

(*Continued*)

My Money: Spending #4

Why?

For what purpose?

For what purpose?

What does that represent?

Now you have your answers! You will likely have some repetitions. Good!

So what do we do with these answers?

VALUES THEMES

Your values are determined by positive and negative influences from the past; you're either trying to avoid something or you're trying to get more of something. So look for patterns that tell you what you've been trying to cut out of your life and what you want to pursue more of.

First, go through and circle everything that matches. Look for repeated words or related ideas/similarities. This helps you identify themes, which will point you to your values.

Second, clarify what those patterns and themes represent.

For example: You might fill your space with beautiful objects and spend time with beautiful people, so you conclude that physical beauty is important to you. What does that really represent? Maybe it's about social prestige, or maybe you're really artistic. Whatever it is, keep questioning until you think you've uncovered it.

Another example: You might spend your time and money on your business. So we can conclude your business matters to you. But what does that really represent? Maybe it's freedom? Maybe it's control? Maybe it's achievement?

This will leave you with a list most likely five to nine items long.

Congratulations! Now they need to be ranked so you can use this set of priorities to determine your decision-making criteria and life priorities. That's what you'll do in the next exercise.

WHEN VALUES COLLIDE: BEING AN EMOTIONALLY SOPHISTICATED WOMAN IN AN EVER-CHANGING LANDSCAPE

It's easy for me to talk about living according to your values, but I haven't always done this well. It's taken me a long time to get to a place where I know how to integrate and feel unapologetic about that.

I think back to when I was in my twenties and had my own marketing agency. A lot of my clients were large corporates. They always assumed I had a boss, because I was so young, and I never corrected them. I just let them treat me like I was less important. And I changed the way I dressed and acted to operate in their corporate world. While I was in marketing I simultaneously had a singing career, and I used a different name and kept it from my clients. Some of them had heard of the singer Claire Trentain and assumed she was my sister, and I never corrected them about that, either.

There was this funny instance where I was performing at a football game as the half-time entertainment, using my stage name, of course. One of my marketing clients was in the crowd and he called me and said, "Oh my God, your sister's up next!" I was backstage ready to go on. The client had told everyone in the corporate box that he knew my sister and he had $500 riding on it. He said, "Can you get her to turn to our corporate box and say hi, and I'll split the money with you?" I thought I was definitely caught—but I got out there, turned to the corporate box and said hi to their accounting firm by name. He still didn't know it was me. And he did give me half the money!

I don't hide that side of myself any more. Now I show up; I know I'm different, I know I use the opposite side of my brain to a lot of my clients. I embrace it and explain to them how that's going to benefit their bottom line.

Recently I had an experience where I ended my working relationship with somebody because she'd done a few things that told me we had a values mismatch. When I had a conversation with her about it she got defensive and tried to talk me out of the reasons I felt we weren't a match, as if they weren't right or didn't matter or something.

That's like when you tell somebody about an emotion you're having and they try to explain why you shouldn't be feeling like that! Your feelings aren't negotiable and neither are your values. You don't have to justify them to anybody who doesn't agree; just recognize that you value different things than they do.

When you start living by your values in every area of life, you're going to run into the problem I mentioned before. The things you value in some areas of your life will inevitably be in conflict with what you value in other areas, which usually means that some areas will get suppressed in favor of others.

For example, it's not unusual for both men and women to compromise on the quality of their family life because they're focused on success at work. In a roundabout way this might actually reflect a high value for family, because they're trying to create long-term financial security for the sake of their partner and kids. But they're compromising the quality of the relationships now in the hope that it pays off long term. This doesn't justify the actions—you are not a success at business if you fail at home.

Sometimes it's fine to let one area edge out another. Sometimes you really do just have to invest in one area short-term, so that you create more freedom and alignment for the long term. That's okay.

But a lot of the time it doesn't *feel* okay. When values are in conflict, it creates guilt and sadness and anger. Most people don't know what to do about it, so they just live with it, but you don't have to live with it. You can create self-awareness around your values and the order in which you prioritize them, to give yourself the best chance of creating a life that has the least amount of friction when it comes to living out your values.

Coaching Exercise: Values Hierarchy

WITH EMILY

From doing the previous exercise, you have a list of values that are important to you. The next step is to decide which order they go in.

First pick the one that rules them all. Knowing this one, you will always be able to say "X is more important than A,B,C, and D!"

Next, go down the list and question every single one in turn. Is freedom more important to you than security, or is security more important than freedom? You'll usually have an emotional reaction that tells you how to place them. If you find yourself feeling that you're not sure—if you don't have a clear emotional response either way—you might have a values conflict.

You'll usually know when your values are in conflict because you'll feel like you're letting yourself down or betraying yourself somehow as you go through your life.

You might have the experiences where you feel guilty doing something, but you wouldn't stop doing it. You're having an emotion that tells you that there's something wrong, but the emotion isn't distressing enough for you to stop. Can you think of a situation in your life right now that feels like that?

It's normal to experience a values conflict when you are rising because your values shift every time you grow. If you're in the process of transitioning out of one mindset and evolving into another one, you'll probably experience a clash between current values and new ones. Most often this can happen around people you share your life with: You still feel a pull to spend time with old friends, but they don't share your new values or support your new goals.

Or you might hold two areas of your life in tension: You love your work and thrive every minute that you're in the office, but as soon as you walk out of the door to go home you feel distressed because you've spent the whole day away from your family, and you feel like you're missing out on your kids.

There's a simple tool you can use to handle conflicting values. It goes like this:

How does pursuing the new value/goal of "X" honor/complement the current value of "Y"?

(Continued)

(Continued)

For example:

"How does putting time into my fitness help me with my freedom?"

"How does working on my budget help me feel more connection
to people I love?"

"How does my spiritual practice help with my security?"

"How does my commitment to work help me contribute to my
family?"

For the last one, the answer might be that you're being an
amazing role model to your children, that you're contributing
financially to their experience of a great life, or that being at
work leaves you energized and inspired so that your kids get
the best version of you when you come home.

Ask yourself the question several times until your brain
spits out a few answers and lands on something satisfying.
You'll know when it's right. You've got a brilliant brain; just keep
asking.

BE A WOMAN, NOT A CHILD

If an area of life isn't working for you, it's most likely because you feel
like you don't have the ability to operate in that area in accordance with
your values. You'll know it's wrong because you'll get negative emotions,
even anxiety and depression.

But guess what? If you've got a values conflict and you can't make it
work, you're most likely operating like a child, not a woman. That's the
cold hard truth. Adults develop the ability to navigate conflicting values
(their own and other people's). That's the definition of maturity.

Grown-ups know how to navigate unfamiliar situations and new
people, in alignment with their values, without feeling really distressed.
That's who I want us all to be—grown-up women who are confident
applying our values, and sophisticated with our own emotions.

That's rising.

CHAPTER **6**

Vision Boards Are Bullshit

How to set effective goals

I love vision boards. I'm an artist, so of course I'm a really visual person.

But so often the way we do vision boards is bullshit. We make it about *this* car or *that* house at the beach. What happens if we don't get that particular thing? Or what if things change and that thing won't bring us happiness anymore? Did we fail?

It's the concreteness of the pictures on vision boards that I have a problem with. Often it's about assets or material things. We cut pictures out of magazines of things that we want and then it's like, we have to get that thing in order to be happy. To achieve our "vision."

I know somebody who has on their vision board *a baby boy.* What the fuck? Does that mean if you have a girl you'll be disappointed? Visual images like that are so definite.

I'm not saying don't have a vision board (like I said, I love them); I'm just saying make your vision board based on your values, not just ideas of things you want to have or achieve. Make your board a mix of words as well as pictures. Include reminders of things that are important to you—photos of people who inspire you, or quotes, or books. A blend of values, assets, and things you want to share with other people as well as things you want to have for yourself. A list of the things that fill your soul. Not a particular address or an exact model of car.

Then anything that comes along—like a new car or whatever—if it excites you, get it. If it ticks the boxes for things that fill your soul—for me that's "fast-paced," "winning," "having nice things"—go for it!

The process of setting the visions and working towards them is more important than whether you actually get all the things or not. You don't know what you don't know—12 months from now your priorities might change and old goals might not seem as important. Put things on Post-it Notes, so you can create a hierarchy and move them around on your board, or even take them off if you change your mind. And make it about your underlying values more than concrete objects or experiences you "have" to have.

Because otherwise you're just going to look up at your vision board and think, "I've failed at half those things. I just gave birth to a girl."

SETTING EFFECTIVE GOALS

As we work through the areas of your life, first you'll identify your values and assess your level of satisfaction in each area. Then in order to increase your satisfaction, you need tools for increasing your effectiveness and the probability of getting what you want out of life. Part of that is knowing how to set effective goals.

Some people think they're not goal-setters. You might be one of them.

Some people just aren't naturally motivated by mapping out goals and working toward them. Other people have tried lots of goal setting in the past and it hasn't worked, so they feel cynical about it.

I'm not interested in putting you through a rigid goal-setting exercise resulting in a plan you'll never stick to, with a vision board made of things that won't really fill up your soul, ultimately leading to insecurity and shame when your plans don't work out. Goal setting should be a source of freedom, not a trap you set for yourself that ends in failure.

Call in the Coach: Emily on Being a Goal Setter

"I'm not a goal setter"

You might not relate to yourself as a goal-setter, but you are one. Everybody is. Our daily lives are a process of setting and achieving thousands and thousands of micro goals. For most people, as soon as they wake up in the morning their first goal is to make it to the toilet (which, if you've given birth to children, isn't a guaranteed achievement!). You achieve that and your brain gives you a little "tick"! All day long you're smashing goals. "Make breakfast and eat it." "Smile at my partner." "Breathe in and out." "Don't fall over."

Notice something about those examples? Most of the goals you work on all day long are unconscious. You don't sit in the car and consciously think "My goal is to drive all the way to work without having an accident"—but your unconscious sure does. Your unconscious is already a goal-setting, goal-smashing superstar.

Your brain's natural ability to manage thousands of micro, unconscious goals can be harnessed to achieve macro, conscious goals. In the past you might have had negative experiences with goals—you can't achieve them, it takes a lot of pain to achieve them, or you don't achieve them the way you planned. We're going to give you a formula for setting effective goals so you'll have a higher probability of achieving them, without a lot of pain and sacrifice, and without having a false attachment to the outcome.

Since your brain is really good at achieving unconscious goals, it follows that the most effective way to set goals is to program them into your unconscious. Our goal-setting formula is going to show you how to do that.

With an effective goal-setting formula you'll create the right kinds of goals: goals that move you in the direction you want to go for the rest of your life. And you'll have a lot of fun along the way.

MOTIVATION

When you ask people what their goals are they'll often talk in terms of what they *don't* want. Have you heard yourself doing that? "I don't want to be stressed about money any more," or "I don't want to miss out on time with the kids."

Everybody does it, but there are two major problems with talking about your goals in terms of what you're trying to get away from.

First, if you're always thinking about what you *don't* want instead of what you *do* want, you've got this negative focus. It fills up your thoughts. "I don't want to be fat any more." "I don't want to be in debt and stressed about money." "I want to stop feeling so lonely." "Fat." "Debt." "Lonely." How are you ever going to achieve anything good if you've got that shit playing in your head all day?

Secondly, if you're motivated to get away from something, once you actually get away from it your motivation disappears. Your brain relaxes and tells you you're fine, so it's really hard to keep going with the behavior you need to maintain your results.

This is how women end up yo-yo dieting. At first you work really hard, go to the gym every day, whatever. Then you start looking different. Your old jeans fit and people are giving you heaps of compliments and you feel really good. That's when you think "yeah, I could eat that whole pizza. I can drink that beer. It's fine, I'm not fat any more!"

So you're wearing your skinny jeans and eating pizza and really enjoying it. Then before you know it, one day your jeans won't zip up and you panic and think "shit, how did I get fat again?" and you get back on the diet. Repeat that for your whole adult life and you've got the experience of a huge majority of women. It's not just dieting; we all have the same experience in all different areas of life. Most of us can think of one goal or one area where we feel like we've tried *everything*. It's like beating your head against a brick wall and you end up thinking that this thing, whatever it is, is just never going to happen for you.

Coaching Exercise: What Are My Motivations?

WITH EMILY

We've defined the problem with setting goals with "away from" motivations (focusing on what we're trying to move away from/avoid).

But if you can set goals with "toward" motivations (focused on what you want to move toward/desire), you can seriously change your life through consistent momentum.

Underneath every away-from motivation there will be a'toward. If you don't want to be stressed about money, find words for what you do want: security, abundance, being well-resourced? If you don't want to be bored at work, imagine what the opposite would feel like. Excited? Appreciated? Challenged?

It might be hard at first, but keep going until you can turn every "don't want" in your life into a "do want." Here's how:

Think about the areas in your life where you're not getting the results you want. Write them down.

Now, be brutal with yourself: Ask yourself "What are the 'away-from' motivations that are driving me in that area?"

Under each area you've written down, fill in this statement.

"I don't want..."

"I don't want..."

"I don't want..."

Now see if you can turn every "I don't want" statement into an "I want" statement. We'll use these statements later in a goal-setting formula. But you can't set effective goals until you know what you want. The question "If I don't want X, what do I want instead?" will work it all out for you!

Use that brilliant mind of yours!

IT'S NOT ABOUT THE GOAL

Before we go any further, I have to tell you something that might piss you off. But stay with me. Here it is:

The main purpose of setting a goal is not *to achieve the goal.*

If you're a perfectionist who loves writing goals and ticking them off, you're probably feeling really uncomfortable right now. What's the point of setting a goal if you're not going to achieve it, right?

If you're somebody who hates working on goals and feels cynical about the whole process, you're probably feeling like this whole chapter has been a waste of time. Why did I spend all that time trying to trick you into setting goals if I was just going to turn around and say it's not about achieving them?

I'm *not* saying that you'll never achieve the goals you set out to, or that it's a bad thing if you do. Obviously it's great to achieve something you wanted.

What I *am* saying is that it's okay, even healthy, to move the goal-posts. You don't have to lock yourself into achieving a goal in exactly the same way, on exactly the particular timeframe, that you intended when you first set it. A good goal will help you improve the consistency and quality of your actions and set you on a great trajectory. That might include achieving the goal exactly the way you planned. But if the goal changes along the way, it's still done its job as long as it's helped you to progress in the direction you want to keep going for the rest of your life.

That's what a really great goal will do. It'll change your behavior so that you're always moving closer to the goals you want to achieve and the kind of person you want to be. If you're anything like me, as you get closer to achieving a goal you'll want to move the goalposts a little further away. So your goals end up evolving as you do, because they're always helping you to perform better and better.

Your goals are your servants, not your master. They're allowed to change as often as you need to adjust them in order to keep moving forward, in alignment with your values.

Call in the Coach: Emily on Results versus Quality Action

One of the things that changed Tamara's businesses so radically was when she started focusing on the quality of her actions rather than the results. When I met Tamara she was running a small business that was doing really well, with an incredible quality of clients—what she was doing with the size of the agency she had was quite unbelievable. But she was running a business that was turning over under a million dollars and she had an A3, size 8 font, border-to-border monthly financial report. It was symptomatic of the way she was way too engrossed in her results,

> *rather than consistency of activity. So we shifted her focus to her activity and that's how she was able to grow the business beyond its previous constraints. And that's how she's grown every other business—by focusing on consistency of activity instead of results.*

A LOCKED-IN GOAL IS A DANGEROUS GOAL

Remember how I said I live my life according to my values, not my plans? Goal setting should operate on the same principle. Because a goal that's not allowed to change assumes that you're not allowed to change either. It's a great way to slow down your personal growth and narrow your opportunities.

If you set all your goals in stone and don't give them any flexibility, you lock yourself into a path that might not actually be right for you by the time you get there. Life changes all the time. Your goals should change too. If you tell yourself you "have" to achieve this or that on a certain timeline, you set yourself up for stress and failure.

It's not just life that changes; you change too. I look back at myself in my twenties, or even myself one year ago, and that person doesn't know what I know now. If I were still determined to achieve all the goals I set for myself 10 years ago, I'd be working off a plan that was right for 10-years-ago me, not the me of today. And I know enough to know that in a year or a decade from now, I'll know a lot more than I do now. The goals I have today might seem silly or limited by then, but if that's the case I will have made some new ones to replace them.

If you're intent on achieving every goal the way you set it, you're not opening yourself up to all the learning and growing and changing you're going to do. You're not allowing for all the possibilities you might see on the way to achieving that goal.

And you're not letting other people in to help or influence or expand the horizons for your goal. You miss all the new connections you could make and all the people you could work with, who will mess your goal around and change it and grow it into something you could never have imagined. That's the magic.

Coaching Exercise: Goal-Setting Formula

WITH EMILY

We've already talked about the fact that your unconscious mind is amazing at achieving goals.

Your conscious mind is passing instructions to your unconscious all the time, and it can't not follow instructions.

You can leverage that process by delivering a goal to your unconscious mind, using the format that it most prefers.

I use an approach adapted from Neurolinguistic Programming (NLP), which you've probably seen a variation of before. To powerfully instruct your unconscious mind, a goal needs to be:

S (specific): in terms of the form it takes, where it occurs in space (place) and when it occurs in time (day, date and year). Don't be lazy! Be specific.

M (measurable): objectively, so that anybody else could measure it.

A ("as if now"): your unconscious operates in the present, so use present tense language.

R (realistic): if it's too unreachable or unbelievable to you, your brain will just delete it.

T (timed): and with a "toward"' motivation, which we talked about earlier.

It also needs to be expressed really simply.

Your unconscious mind has the cognitive capacity of a seven-year-old, so you need to imagine you are giving instructions to your seven-year-old self. Really clear and simple.

Here's the formula you can use for setting your most powerful goals.

Each goal has three parts. For each goal, fill in this three-part statement.

1. *Time/present.* It is now _____ [day, date, year]
2. *Realistic, measurable result.* I have/am/see _____ [your specific, measurable, toward outcome]
3. *Your toward reaction.* I am _____ [your physical/ emotional/mental reaction].

For example:

It is now Friday, the 21st of January, 2022.

I am opening the front door of our new home with the new keys.

I'm grinning and I'm saying to myself, "I'm so excited to be living in this house!"

It is now Monday, the 17th of July, 2023.

I am looking at my EOFY statements and the profit says $1,200,000.

I punch the sky and I feel on top of the world.

It is now Saturday, the 20th of November, 2021.

I am pressing "stop" on my fitness watch and the screen shows a time of 25:00 for my 5k run.

I feel powerful and proud.

Part 2, the result, is the hardest part to write. Ask yourself—how will you measure whether you've achieved the goal? How could somebody else measure it? Does it need to be in writing? In numbers? In an observable activity? A tangible interaction with another human being that they could also verify? The only rule is it can't be measured in feelings.

If part 2 were written as a feeling, it might look like this (these are examples of what *not* to do):

It is now Monday, the 17th of July, 2023.

I am so happy that we made a profit of $1.2 million this year.

(Continued)

(Continued)

or

It is now Saturday, the 17th of November, 2021.
I feel amazing after a 5k run.

See the difference? In the examples above, there was nothing material or tangible to visualize as proof of the goal—it was based on a feeling. Save the feelings for part 3, where you imagine the reaction you'll have to achieving the concrete result in part 2.

So for a tangible part 2, you might imagine yourself telling another person about the goal you've achieved, reading a report about it, receiving a certificate, holding a photograph of yourself having done it, the numbers off a screen, and so on.

Rewrite your goal three or four times until you come up with the briefest, clearest version possible.

Once you've written out the goal, check in with how you feel about it. If you feel uncomfortable with it or don't believe it will happen, it won't work. Your brain will do what's called a deletion and disregard it. If this happens, you need to write it differently or set a different goal.

It's okay to set goals that stretch your limits, but you need to have a certain amount of "I don't know how this is going to happen, but I'm excited and open to it."

If you repeatedly struggle to believe in the goals you're setting, you'll probably benefit from going to a coach and doing some work around your mindset.

WHAT ABOUT GOALS THAT HAVE NO TANGIBLE OUTCOME?

In the years leading up to the release of this book, cumulative practice has become a hot commodity. Everybody is raving about morning routines, daily rituals, and meditation habits. If you have a goal to do something daily, that's a cumulative goal.

The opposite type of cumulative goal is when you're trying to avoid something or break a bad habit—for example, you might set a goal to go 30 days without drinking alcohol.

Or you might have a goal to bring about positive change in an area of your life, for example: being a good parent, experiencing regular loving connection with your partner, developing a new discipline or using more empowering self-talk.

There's an advanced technique for that kind of goal setting; it's something that we recommend you explore with a coach.

ONE FINAL WORD OF WARNING

Don't attach your goal to external rewards; let the goal you set be the reward. You can work out another way to reward yourself—this specific exercise needs to stay clean of other contaminants.

Here's an example of goal contamination:

I had a client who said to me, "When I achieve this company target, I'm going to reward myself with that new car. I would never buy that car for myself unless I achieved that goal."

Guess what? A short time later, their existing car blew up and they had to get a new one. Of course they purchased the car that they said was only supposed to be a reward! I'm not going to make any comment about how those circumstances lined up, but they did.

Remember, your unconscious is like a sassy seven-year-old who's been promised a lollipop if they do their chores. It will always prefer to find a way to get the lollipop without the work!

So if you hear yourself saying that you can reward yourself (e.g. with a car) when you achieve that goal (e.g., a company target), save yourself a lot of cognitive hassle, tell the truth to yourself, and just make the car the goal.

(Continued)

(Continued)

WHAT TO DO WITH YOUR GOALS ONCE YOU'VE WRITTEN THEM

Once you've written down your goals using the formula above, you need to engage with them on a regular basis. Ways you could do this:

- Stick them up on your mirror.
- Read them every morning when you're planning your day.
- Review them once a week.
- If you're in a mastermind group, read them out loud and share them regularly.
- Work with a coach to install them unconsciously.

FREE YOURSELF FROM GOALS

Just like your plans, your goals might change. And once you get close to achieving a goal that you'll probably lose interest in, move the goalposts a little further away and set a better one (at least that's what I do).

Goal setting is not about ticking off a list of achievements—it's about honing your skills, achieving more stuff with less effort, increasing your options, and growing all the time in the direction you want to go. *It's not about the goal.* So you can let it go. Freedom!

CHAPTER **7**

It's All About the Journey

How and why to write your bucket list

There's an exercise you can do (that runs on a similar principle to the goal-setting exercise from Chapter 6) where you talk as though it's a date in the future, and you describe your life in as much detail as possible. *It's the year 2040 and I'm sitting in a room filled with luxurious furniture and pieces of art and I have two children blah blah blah.*

That can be a great exercise to do. But I think you'd write it differently every 10 years, wouldn't you? God, mine changes every year.

Instead of describing what's around you in that type of long-term exercise, I'd say go *inward*. Talk about your values and how you're living them out, not about tangibles like what type of room you're sitting in. *The year is 2040. I'm blessed to still have my health because I've looked after myself. I'm content and I sleep well at night because I haven't burned any bridges. I failed at a lot of things but I know I always gave 100%. I love being older and I have no wish to be 20 again.* That's what mine would sound like right now (but ask me another day and I'd probably say something different).

When I talk about not getting too attached to concrete goals, I'm talking about big-picture life goals—ideas like "I will be worth this many dollars when I'm 40" or "I will retire at this particular age" or "I will be surrounded by my three children who haven't been born yet." You can't necessarily plan those things or know that they'll still be right for you in the future.

So that's what I think about life goals: Don't go too concrete, live in accordance with your values, and know that the specifics might change.

On the other hand, the place you're allowed to be as concrete as you want is your bucket list.

Your bucket list is just a list of great stuff that you want to do or have in your life. These can definitely be specific things! You know you might not get around to doing all of them, or you might change your list as you think of new things. It's fine. It's meant to be fun!

When you're an entrepreneur, you lose more often than you win. So for me and a lot of entrepreneurs I know, having a bucket list is our way of making it work. While we're chasing achievements or living through down times in our businesses we're having a lot of great experiences along the way. It really makes it about the journey, not the endgame.

There are lots of people out there with websites and resources to help you make your bucket list. Everybody has different takes. I personally love the work of Keith Abraham and I recommend his approach for making a bucket list.[1]

A lot of people get stuck when they first try to think of things to put on their list. Keith has a great resource that gives you 25 questions to ask to help you brainstorm a list of 100 things you'd like to do in your lifetime.

He also goes deeper and gives you eight categories that cover most of your life. Then he encourages you to think of lifetime dreams you want to achieve in each area. The life categories in my book are slightly different, but we'll do the same thing. As we work through each area of life in the following chapters, there'll be an opportunity for you to add items to your bucket list for the area covered in each chapter.

THE BEAUTY OF SHARING YOUR BUCKET LIST

I'm in a chapter of Entrepreneurs' Organization, and one of our things is that everybody has a bucket list. We share our lists with each other so we can help each other achieve them. One of my bucket list items was to meet Richard Branson, and somebody in EO said they had a ticket to go on his spaceship and they could arrange for me to meet him. Another one of my dreams was to have a business that was valued at more than $10 million in under two years and my EOers said right, let's teach you about sweat equity. (And I got there, but that's a whole other book.)

But then I thought, *What a hypocrite. I'm out here having all these experiences and my team is back in the office running my business.* They were all working hard so that I could achieve my dreams. What about theirs?

So I entrenched the bucket list into my company culture. Everyone on my team has 100 dreams. They've all written them down. Part of my executive assistant's job is to make sure that every time a new team member starts, they write their list—then I go through and highlight all the ones I can make possible because of my network.

My rule is that everybody has to make four of their dreams happen every year. I get my four, everybody on my team gets their four, and everybody wins.

Here's my current bucket list as inspiration (remember, no judgment):

1. Marry Florian with the girls and K there.
2. Meet Richard Branson.
3. Walk the German Rhine tour with the family.
4. Own an original Matisse artwork (not a print).
5. Buy and renovate a house with no budget restraints.
6. Have my best-ever body in my forties.
7. Write a #1 song.
8. Spend six months in Europe and six months in Australia (house swap).
9. Have a beach house and a pied-à-terre unit in the city.
10. Practice bikram yoga three times a week and do all poses 100%.
11. Own a Maserati while I still look hot in it.
12. Have a white Christmas.
13. Hold an art exhibition of my own original art.
14. Every school holiday, work from home and the beach.
15. Help and spend time with Thai orphan children.
16. Go to Africa and witness a gorilla family in the wild.
17. Live until I'm 80-plus.
18. Never be bankrupt, always be cash-flow positive.
19. Have a cellar with wine collected from around the world.
20. Write a book that empowers more women in business.
21. Take kids on a trip/vacation away alone each year.
22. Swim with whale sharks.
23. Rio Carnival Mardi Gras celebrations.
24. Cherry blossoms with K.

25. See the pyramids and Great Sphinx of Giza.
26. Race an Aston Martin (10 hot laps).
27. Have a photo book each year.
28. Go to the Melbourne Open finals.
29. Fly business class always.
30. Birthing of Giants program: EMP Boston graduate.
31. Be one of the top 100 Australian businesses.
32. Be one of the top five fastest-growing Australian businesses.
33. Grow and sell a company for $50M+ in less than five years.
34. Be a worldwide professional speaker once semi-retired.
35. Give $1 million to charity per year.
36. Have a profitable company that doesn't need me in it.
37. Make $10,000 a week from my assets.
38. See the ancient wonders of the world.
39. See jazz live in the top four places in the world.
40. Drink alcohol on weekends only for 12 months straight.
41. Have an executive assistant and not look at all my emails.
42. Be in the top 10 female entrepreneurs globally.
43. Have a trackside tent at the Melbourne Cup (and helicopter in).
44. Hot springs (natural onsen) at Zaborin in Japan.
45. Say no more than I say yes.

START YOUR OWN LIST!

As we walk through each area of life in this book, I'll encourage you to stop and add some items to your bucket list. Here's the first space to do that.

Remember to base it on your values, dream big, and have fun!

Building Your Bucket List: Self

The first section of your bucket list is going to be about *you*. Not in a selfish way; in fact, this section could definitely include things you want to do with your loved ones.

But there will be space in later chapters to think specifically about bucket list items you want to create around your marriage or romantic life, your kids (if you have them), your extended family, and your friends. There will also be space later to think of things you want to do for your community, for the less fortunate, or for global causes.

Right now it's about you and the things that fill your soul.

If you're not sure where to start, flip to Chapter 8 and think about the things that fill up your soul. Use those things as a starting point, and let them inspire you to write down some things you'd like to do in your lifetime—things that help you feel more like yourself.

Examples to get you started:

Buy a holiday house to escape the city.

Plant and maintain a garden.

Join a book club.

See friends on a weekly basis no matter how busy I am (or how messy the house is).

Meditate for 20 minutes a day.

Cook a different dish once a month.

Go on a three-day retreat once a year to refocus alone.

Buy myself fresh flowers once a week.

Travel to a new overseas location once a year.

MY BUCKET LIST: THINGS TO DO FOR MYSELF

1. _____
2. _____
3. _____
4. _____
5. _____
6. _____

(Continued)

(*Continued*)

7. _____

8. _____

9. _____

10. _____

NOTE

1. When it comes to your building your bucket list, a great place to start is with Keith Abraham's online resources, available at https://keithabraham.com/free-resources/.

CHAPTER **8**

Filling Up Your Soul

How to stay stable and ride the roller coaster

When I was pregnant I noticed people loved the saying, "Happy mom, happy baby."

But I got a bit annoyed because I thought, why does that only apply when you're breastfeeding or have a newborn? Isn't it always "happy mom, happy kids"?

And why does it only apply to moms? What about "happy me, happy marriage" or "happy home, happy business"?

And why is it that we only look after our health when we have an event to go to, or when we want to look good for something, like a wedding?

Those things annoy me. Making your health a priority only when it's on show. Focusing on your well-being only if you're in a special time of life, like having a baby.

I think looking after yourself has to be a constant. Sometimes, when you're busy with other priorities, you find yourself varying from the constant. That's when you recognize that you're getting a bit off-kilter and need to get yourself back on track. But it's always something that needs to be there, underneath everything else. This is your foundation.

So I have this baseline level of well-being, of feeling okay, of being myself. The level that I set for myself is about what I give myself permission to be worthy of.

And I know when I'm not there. I know the warning signs that tell me I'm not doing well, and I know what to expect when I let certain things slide.

Finally, I know how to reset myself to where I need to be. I don't look to Florian or my friends or my coach to get my balance back. I just have these things that I've learned over time, that work for me. I know when I do them I'll get closer to that basic level of happiness and feeling like myself.

That's what we're going to go through in this chapter. Where's your baseline? How do you know when you're not there? How do you get it back?

YOUR PERSONAL PIE

We all know what it feels like when the blend is right. You have enough energy to get through most things you want to achieve in a day, and when you get home on Friday night and it's time to sit on the couch with a glass of wine, you feel like you can really enjoy it. When you think about work you feel a buzz of motivation and you can't wait to check how things are performing, because you know they're going well. You look forward to going home to your family. You have time to have a bit of fun.

The blend looks different for everybody. You might be at your most content when you're working fewer hours and spending more time at home with the kids, but another person might thrive on 14-hour work-days. Your ideal week might involve going to the gym five times, but another person will feel great about a massage.

So it's up to you to define your own ideal. Ask yourself, "When am I at my most content?"

To answer this question, imagine your life as a pie. You have a slice for work, a slice for holidays, a slice for time at home, a slice for time with friends, and all the other ways you mainly spend your time. How big do you want each slice to be?

It might help to think about the slices not as chunks of time, but chunks of energy. How much of your focus and attention do you want to be taken up with your business? With your kids? With your social life? With your current hobby, obsession, or personal challenge?

And how small do you need to make the slices of things you *don't* particularly want in your life, but can't avoid?

An example for me is doing chores. You can't go through life never cleaning up anything, but I want my chores slice to be about 1%. I literally just want to pick up after myself; I get annoyed picking up after my children and I draw the line at picking up after my husband. I will not cook and I will not clean. I don't enjoy it, and I could be doing something I love for half an hour to pay for it instead of doing it myself and taking four hours to get it done. That's what I know about me and chores.

So when you're at your most content, how big is each slice of energy in your pie?

When you've figured this out, you might take some of the main slices and divide them up again, according to what makes you most content in those areas. For example, I know that I function best when my work slice is at least 50% creative work and no more than 10% on compliance and reporting and all that "sleep-at-night" shit. I can handle more of that if it's motivational and related to the creative stuff; the more I'm winning, the longer I can look at a report. I'm happy if I can tweak the numbers and grow things. But in general, about 10% is my limit. I know that about myself.

In my personal life slice, I need one day a week that's all about me—my friends, my children, the activities we like to do. Absolutely no obligations whatsoever. I work during the week and I work long hours; that's fine, it's a big chunk of my life and I love it. But it means that I guard my weekends really carefully. The kids don't do sports on the weekend; they can do as many activities as they like during the week after school, but we don't do sports on weekends. We don't have pets because we love to travel on the weekends and overseas at least twice a year (and we wouldn't want to put our pets in a kennel). Travel is a huge part of keeping me and my hubby sane; if I personally don't go over the ocean at least once every two months I get island fever. And sleep-ins are really important to my well-being, at least one sleep-in a week with cuddles. That's me.

So ask yourself: When are you happiest at work? What activities are you doing? Are you mentoring people, are you strategizing, are you coming up with ideas or executing them?

When are you happiest at home? What activities are you doing? Are you cleaning, are you present with your kids, are you cooking with your family, are you out in your garden?

This exercise is about self-awareness. Once you can define your perfect pie, you know what you need to do to keep your baseline steady. It's not up for judgment because everybody's got their own thing. It's your game and you get to define the rules. Heck, I've never had a gym membership, and I count massage as part of my exercise time!

If you're off-kilter, it can take a while to change your habits to where you want them to be. But it's worth the investment to get back on track. I don't try to fix everything at once. I'll figure out which area is the furthest from where it needs to be and go and fix that.

Getting this right can seem overwhelming, but everyone's always got options. My favorite saying is that you're only one decision away from changing your life. We're all guilty of overcomplicating things, me included.

For instance, I had a situation where I downsized my role in my own company, took on a new CEO to replace myself, and went from earning $200,000 a year as CEO to $80,000 in a part-time marketing role. That might sound crazy, but I knew that I couldn't stay heavily involved in that business because it had grown to a size where what it needed from me wasn't creativity. It needed a whole other level of management that would mean my work slice wasn't anywhere near the 50% of creative work that I need to maintain my baseline.

It was great that I knew which bus stop to get off at. (Usually you don't know until you've passed it, so unfortunately you often need to go through that experience to determine when to press the exit button.) But reducing my salary created a new problem: Namely, how do we pay our living expenses?

So I thought about my options:

I could save money by not having a cleaner, somebody who irons my clothes and does all my chores. That's one way to save $300 a week. *But I hate doing chores.*

Another way would be to send Florian to work. I could say, "It's your turn now." But that would mean me having to look after the kids' after-school activities and do the school run. *More chores!*

Either of those options would bring us back to neutral, financially. *But, chores!*

The other way to get us back to neutral would be for me to earn more. I could go out and find more creative projects that pay. But fee-for-service didn't serve my small business passion, as I would be working on other people's businesses, not mine.

Alternatively I could sell some assets and grant myself the time to explore my next business adventure. So that's what I did. I know I return more than property does, I was still meeting my commitments to the family and their current lifestyle, and I got the space to reinvent.

Some people get the seven-year itch—I get the four-year itch in business, you could say.

I guess I could happily have chosen to stick to working three days a week at work and done more housework. That'd be a great option for some people, who might hate the idea of having to start a new job and opt to do more at home.

It's not a question of whether work is *better* than chores or whether assets are *more important* than self-investment. Plenty of people would be happy working less and doing the chores. I know myself well enough to know I'm not one of those people. It's about *me* understanding what makes *me* happy in life.

PEOPLE WHO GET IT

I've mentioned that I belong to my local chapters of Entrepreneur's Organization and Young President's Organization. In both EO and YPO, every member gets assigned to a Forum: a small group of peers who meet up once a month, confidentially, for support and advice. Forum is a place where you can share the parts of your life that nobody else understands. Your family and friends might be supportive, but unless they're also running multiple businesses, or trying to solve a problem that's never been tackled before, or tap into a new industry—unless they share that particular blend of personality traits that make up an entrepreneur—they probably don't completely get it.

If you're an entrepreneur, I can't recommend EO highly enough. If that isn't for you, find an organization that meets your needs. You might get the most value out of a community that's specifically for women in business, or for creative people in your industry, or whatever your personal situation is. Look for a group of people who are going through the same thing, and meet with them for reflection and accountability. They'll be a good sounding board when you're not content, and offer insight from their own experiences to help you get back on track.

THINGS THAT FILL UP YOUR SOUL

While I was writing this book, a friend of mine was going through a lot of shit in his business. I was having a bit of a shitty time too, going through a transition with my own business that meant I was doing hardly any creative work. Both of us are normally positive people who are used to loving our work and basically feeling like we are winning all the time, which made this time extra hard to deal with. It was really wearing us both down and—what do you know—throwing other parts of our pie out.

So I said to him, "We need to pick our top five things that are inexpensive ways to relieve stress and get us back to thinking and performing at our best." (Not just as leaders at work, but also as good parents and nice people who smile at other people on the train.) We agreed that we'd be each other's buddies and make sure that we did at least one thing every couple of weeks.

I think of these things as things that fill up my soul.

When it comes to physical health, we know that prevention is better than cure. I actually think the same thing applies across all parts of your life, whether it be your marriage, your mental health, or your sense of self. The things that fill up your soul are the things that need to happen to prevent you from getting burned out or being a crappy parent or resentful partner. It might feel self-indulgent, but it's probably your best work.

The things that fill up your soul are things you can do for yourself, without depending on other people to make you feel better. That doesn't make other people redundant; it's just that it's important to know how to maintain your own baseline without relying on other people to tell you when you're off-kilter. The people close to you will be able to sense when you're not doing your best, but only you know when you really need to do something about it.

When you're figuring out what fills up your soul, here are a few things to keep in mind:

- *Remember times when you were really content and happy.* Write all those moments down and then look for common denominators. Did you have a lot of happy moments near the ocean? Did a lot of your best times involve your children? Whatever it is, just notice it.
- *Don't do things that you think will make you happy because they work for other people.* When my friend and I agreed to keep each other

accountable for doing the things on our lists, he sent me a text at 5 a.m. with a picture of the sunrise. Getting up early fills up *his* soul, whereas I love sleeping in. For lots of people their "me time" is going to get their nails done, but I'd rather have ugly nails then go through that experience. It takes too long and it smells awful. Don't expect your things to fill my soul or my things to fill yours. Your list is like your DNA. It's unique to you and you can't change it.

- *Don't make excuses.* Include some things on your list that don't cost any money, some things that don't take much time, and some things that you can do alone without relying on other people. That way you can always find something to do, even if you have limited resources.

- *Make sure your list covers different areas of life, and that at least some of the things are within your own control.* It's okay if some things on your list are business related (mine are), but you can't tie all your happiness to success at work. You can't wrap everything on your list around your children. A lot of life isn't in your control, so you have to find happiness in all different places. Your list should reflect that.

There's no judging your list; it just *is*. Mine includes things like:

The ocean

Making memories

A clean, organized home

Growing startups

Time with the kids

Music

Travel

Winning in business

Massage (don't save that shit for a birthday present!)

Being appreciated

Time with K (my best friend)

Creative marketing & strategy

Looking good

Giving gifts

Mentoring and coaching

Last weekend I said to my girls, "Guess what fills Mommy's soul? Music. I love music and I want to do something with you and music."

They'd recently told me that they didn't know who Elvis Presley was. That sparked an idea for a project we could do together. I got so excited; I hadn't been this excited about anything in a long time. I decided I'd introduce them to all the legends of music. We made a poster and wrote them all on it—The Beatles, The Rolling Stones, Elton John, David Bowie (spelled "David Bonie" by my six-year-old). One night a week we were going to do a disco night, watch the DVDs, dance (jump around), "move like Mick Jagger," and play the records really loud. It was something that I came up with myself, that wasn't going to take me a lot of effort, and that would last the next six weekends. The process of planning it made me happy in an instant.

Understand me when I say it *really* can be anything that fills up your soul and it's *really* not up for judgment.

So first you make a list. Then you look to yourself to actually do those things. And then you have to communicate it to the people around you, so they understand why you need to do it.

Seriously, it's important to share your list with the people in your life who can help you fill up your soul, whether it be your partner, your kids (if they're old enough), or your best friend. It's not selfish or self-centered; if somebody loves you, you're doing them a favor by making it really easy for them to show you: If you've told them, "do these five things and that'll make me happy," how easy is that for them?

You can do the exercise together, so that you know what fills up their soul, too. It's a bit like that theory of the Five Love Languages. Everybody speaks a different "language" that makes them feel loved: You might need lots of cuddles or quality time while I like verbal affirmation, not gifts. (I love giving other people gifts but I don't really care about receiving them.) In the same way, everybody has a different language for what fills up their soul. Find out what makes each of you feel happy, so you can do it for each other.

WHEN YOU'RE STUCK

Sometimes one slice of your pie is way smaller or bigger or made of different layers than you want it to be, but you can't fix it right away. I don't usually say things like "can't" because I believe you've always got options, but sometimes there are really pressing circumstances—like somebody's died or been fired. Sometimes in business you don't have a choice except do the shit you have to do to turn it around. That's fine. Whatever the reason, sometimes you're trapped by circumstances that you can't impact right away.

This is when it's especially important to fill up your soul in all the other areas. When I found myself stuck in that situation where I was only doing 10% creative work (until I could exit), we all knew why I wasn't doing well. Work is this giant chunk of my life and I wasn't doing the part of it that makes me happy. Florian empathized but he said, "Well, I can't do anything about that." Yes, you can! Don't buy me flowers, man! Review my list!

Flowers won't fix a work problem, but coming home to a clean house instead of a messy one, not having to book the cleaner myself, knowing that Florian has organized a nice family experience for the weekend—that makes a difference. When I'm suffering in one area he can do stuff in other areas. If you get to the end of a weekend and your soul is really full, not depleted by doing more shit you don't want to do, you can face the office on Monday morning.

That's true whether you've got someone supporting you at home or whether you're filling up your soul all by yourself. So when you find yourself feeling stuck:

- Identify the problem.
- Ask yourself: Do I have an action plan? Is there hope or am I sitting in it until I can find a solution?
- Either way, revert to the list of what fills your soul and start doing more of it.

MENTAL WELLNESS

In 2015–2016 I was the president of my local chapter of Entrepreneurs Organization. During my year as president I'd managed to put good reserves of cash in the bank to benefit the year ahead. So we had this extra money and they asked me what I wanted to spend it on. I think they were like, "We've got 10 thousand extra dollars—do you want to have a bigger party?" That's basically what they expected me to do! (Fair enough—I do love a good party.)

But I didn't. At the party, at which I was the outgoing president, I made my thank you speech. I also said this:

> According to Forbes, only 7% of the general population suffer from depression but a whopping 30% of founders report dealing with its effects.[1]
>
> Entrepreneurship is a deeply personal journey. It's incredibly difficult to separate your individual identity from your business, so business setbacks end up as personal setbacks. Depression can quickly take root.
>
> We need to accept that setbacks will outnumber successes. Most days will be stressful. The game we chose to play, and the ability to embrace these realities, is what makes the people in this room so extraordinary.
>
> Thank God for Forum. When you hit these moments you have your group to go to. But we're not experts in psychology. Entrepreneurs need to be able to reach out and get help when they need it, which is difficult in a world where we want to be "winning." Asking for help is not a weakness and we need to change the mentality around this.
>
> So I am so proud to announce that the board has unanimously agreed to a 10-thousand-dollar budget to provide these services to any one of us when this time arises.

So we had 10 thousand dollars to cover mental health services for any member who needed it and was willing to ask. Later that night after I made the speech, somebody came up to me in confidence and told me that he'd suffered from depression for a long time in the past. He said, "This would have been really helpful for me. I'll give you another two grand."

Then somebody else came up to me and said basically the same thing. And somebody else. And here I was thinking I'd been talking to a bunch of boys who wouldn't care about my speech. It was nice to be wrong.

By the end of the night another announcement was made. Through donations made in the past two hours, we'd doubled the funds.

THE WEIGHT OF BEING AN ENTREPRENEUR

The fact of the matter is this: If you're driven, an entrepreneur, a type-A personality, or a hundred other things, mood swings are part of your genetic hardwiring. It's a blessing and a curse.[2]

—Tim Ferriss

In my generation, mental health is something that we've started to explore as we get a little bit older. When I was growing up it wasn't talked about as much as it is now; we threw pills at the problem as opposed to having conversations and research and support. I'm pretty sure the entrepreneurs of the future are going to be much better equipped than we are.

I think the mental health conversation is really important for entrepreneurs. We're natural risk-takers, and the risks don't always pay off. We're high achievers, which means we put ourselves under a lot of pressure to excel all the time. We thrive on winning, but quite often we lose. All of this means our mental state is a pressure cooker that could explode if we don't keep letting off steam.

And you don't win if you're not confident; you need to feel like a winner to win. I'm not one for putting on a brave face and faking it until you make it. So how do you maintain that state of confidence, when in general you lose more than you win in this game?

Accept that your business is always going to be a roller coaster. You're kidding yourself if you think you'll ever get to the point where you're winning all the time and you can relax. "After we launch this product" or "Once we get investors" or "When we're turning over this many dollars"... no. There will always be ups and downs. That's just the way it is. You're going to be on a roller coaster whatever you do, so you need to learn how to ride it.

If you tie your business (or your career) to your personal identity, you're going to feel the highs and lows deeply, and like I said there are usually more lows than highs. If you let them define you, you've lost. So for me it's about how to enjoy the roller coaster without letting it throw me around too much. I need to keep my personal state more stable.

Your business can't be your source of mental wellness. Your marriage can't be your source of mental wellness. Your children can't be your source of mental wellness. All of those things can be sources of contentment and energy and happiness at different times, but you need to know you'll be okay if you're not winning in any of those areas.

That doesn't mean you shut those relationships out and don't rely on them; it just means that you are responsible for your own stability. It's your job to reset yourself when you feel yourself getting off track. That's when you come back to assessing your blend and doing the things that fill up your soul.

As with all types of health, when it comes to mental health, prevention is better than a cure. The things I'm talking about, filling up your soul and staying on track, are preventative measures.

Saying that makes it sound easy. And women tend to be really good at just getting on with life and making it *look* easy. But it takes its toll. How do you communicate to people around you when you're struggling?

If you find yourself struggling to keep your head above water, ask for help. Most of us could benefit from professional support at one point in our lives or another. We outsource everything else—somebody to clean our house, train us at the gym, do our hair, deliver our groceries—why not get help with our mental wellness too?

As an entrepreneur or ambitious woman, your mind is your most important tool. Staying on track and filling up your own soul is your most important work; the quality of your personal state determines the quality of everything else you do. So make it a priority.

WARNING SIGNS

If this whole chapter is about self-awareness, there's one more thing to be aware of. I already said it's important to notice what it feels like when you're going well, so you can keep coming back to that state. It's also equally important to notice the things that tell you when you're not doing well, so that you can do something about it before things get too rough.

Everyone struggles sometimes and everyone reverts to bad habits when they're under pressure. We all fall on a shovel but it depends how deep you want to dig the hole. Once you're in it, everything else starts to fall in with it. Your marriage falls in the hole, your work, your relationships. Everything goes in that hole, so you really don't want to fall in.

Be mindful of the things that do and don't work for you when you're on the edge.

When I've got a shovel in my hand, I have to limit alcohol. I know that it doesn't serve me very well when I'm feeling low. The way I interact with alcohol can be an indication of how well I'm going at the moment, so I keep an eye on it.

Another bad sign for me is isolation. If I go quiet, my best friend Kylie calls my husband. "What's happened at work? She's not returning my calls, she hasn't made plans for the weekend, something's going on." That's not a good sign for me; I know that about myself and the people close to me know it.

When I'm not myself I don't accept speaking gigs. I think it's because I feel like I'm losing and I don't have the authority to go and tell people to be successful. That's another sign that I'm not doing well.

Be mindful of the things that you do when you're not yourself. A lot of women hear themselves get bitchier. Some people throw other people under buses. Some people take it out on their partners or kids. Some people have affairs. Some people can't be alone with themselves, always hosting people and filling up their home. Whatever it is for you, just notice the things that make you think, hmmm, maybe I'm not doing so well.

Then figure out the problem.

Share with the people closest to you.

Make a plan.

Go fill up your soul.

COACHING BREAK

When I talk about the category of Self, I'm thinking about spiritual, emotional, intellectual, and physical health—the things you carry inside yourself, that determine who you are, and impact whether you're thriving or struggling.

Emily has designed an exercise to help you thrive in each of those four areas. Take some time to identify what you need in each area, and that will help you to know how to fill up your soul.

Some areas will be more interesting or important to you. And you'll probably be doing better in some areas than others already.

So here we've included the exercises for your *spiritual, emotional,* and *physical* health. You can do all three right away, or start with the one that calls to you most. Use these as tools to come back to when you need to reset in one of these areas.

When you're ready to think about *intellectual* growth, head over to Chapter 9.

SPIRITUAL

Coaching Exercise: What Do I Belong To?

WITH EMILY

Spirituality is something bigger than you; it is what you feel you belong to.

The purpose of this exercise is to support you in an important and often overlooked area. How to feel spiritually fulfilled.

Spirituality doesn't have to be complicated, deep or involve a lot of struggle. It's a really simple thing: What do I belong to? What bigger system does my identity sit within? What do I choose to be a part of?

Most people belong to multiple systems. Your spirituality is not necessarily defined by a single overarching system, like the religious or philosophical view you use to frame the world (although if you do have one that you ascribe to, this would be high on the list).

Step 1. "What do I belong to?"

Write a list that describes your own spirituality: a list of the things that you belong to, that give you a sense of belonging.

For example, this is how I (Emily) define mine: I belong to my family of origin and my family of creation (my husband and daughter). I belong to the natural environment. I belong to humanity. I belong to Australia. I belong to the motherhood, the sisterhood, and a community of empowered women. When I play sports I belong to my team and club. Finally, I am in a female business community where I also experience belonging.

When you've written your own list, divide it into "unconditional" and "conditional."

Unconditional systems are things that you belong to without condition. You don't need anybody to validate your membership. Your belonging to it doesn't depend on opportunity or material circumstances. For example, belonging to "humanity" or "nature" is something that can't be taken away from me.

For many people, belonging to their country of origin or the country they live in is pretty close to unconditional. For some of us, belonging to our family of origin feels secure enough that we'd say it's unconditional, but for other people this isn't true. (If you've got a really messy family of origin, it's okay to stop seeing it as a source of spiritual belonging.)

Conditional systems are things that you choose to belong to and where your belonging depends on the approval of others or on other conditions that you have to uphold. For example, being on a sports team is a spiritual experience for some people, and there's a requirement that you pay a membership fee and maintain a certain level of ability to stay on the team. This is a conditional belonging.

A rising person will have a good mix of conditional and unconditional belongings. If all the things you belong to are conditional, you're in a precarious space spiritually, because your total sense of identity and belonging depends on a bunch of things that could be taken away by others. Not great in the security stakes. All unconditionals will have us feeling connected but not particularly special. No fun. Blending, again, is required here!

_____   _____
_____   _____
_____   _____
_____   _____
_____   _____

(Continued)

(*Continued*)

Step 2. Fill my cup.

Once you've got the list that feels right to you, write a parallel list. For each item on your list, write down ways you could take actions to fulfill yourself in that area.

Then do those things regularly. For example, you may feel you belong to the physical world (get out of your head) when you do yoga—great! How often do you need to do yoga to feel that awesome connection? The blending advantage here is that you probably also get physical and emotional benefits too. Three for one? Yes, please!

One of the biggest impacts I believe EO and the experience of forum and global events has had on Tamara is giving her a stimulating and structured regular set of activities where she very much belongs! "Turns out I'm not an alien—there is a tribe of us!" she acclaims.

To sum up, this is how to give yourself the best chance of being a spiritually fulfilled person:

1. Define what you belong to (this is a chance to shed old stuff too!).
2. Be aware of the things that help you feel fulfilled in each belonging.
3. Make those actions regular practises.

EMOTIONAL

Coaching Exercise: Dealing with Emotions

WITH EMILY

Want to be powerful? Want to be cool under pressure? Want to not regret your reactions? Want to make your decisions from your awesomeness instead of your stress or anger?

Below I've given you a set of steps for processing the six major negative emotions: anger, sadness, fear, hurt, guilt, and shame. These are the ones that haunt us, burn us out, make us bitter, cynical, tired, and unclear.

Every emotion has a unique job; each one embodies a message that tells you what's "wrong." It's your job to listen and understand. I've included the "message" of each emotion here so you can process your feelings and when that happens they are eased.

I've also included the spectrum of each emotion, to help you identify what you're feeling. We have a complex emotional range—you might not realize that FOMO is a kind of sadness or that yes, that feeling of being very slightly ticked off is anger that might need to be processed. The spectrum is there to help you understand what type of emotional reaction you're having, so that you know which steps to follow.

Your task is to pick something in your life that provokes a negative, unwanted emotional reaction. Identify the emotion (is it anger, sadness, fear, hurt, guilt, or shame?), then work through the steps for processing that emotion, until it feels resolved.

You'll know it's dealt with properly when the feeling goes away. If you reach the end of the process and the emotion is still hanging around, it needs more work or hasn't been identified correctly. Go back and try again! The negative feeling tells you that this thing is still important and needs to be dealt with.

This isn't necessarily an exercise you have to do right this minute, but a tool for you to come back to with any emotion that you need to process.

ANGER

Message: "A rule or boundary has been crossed."

Rules and boundaries represent safety. Anger tells us that our safety has been threatened; this is why we get pissed off when people don't use their turn signal in traffic, even they

(Continued)

(*Continued*)

were three cars ahead and didn't impact us at all. When you feel unsafe, it's normal to try to regain your safety by exercising power over others or the situation, running away, or wanting to punish the person who crossed the line. These are all anger reactions.

Spectrum: From "a little bit ticked off" to "uncontrollable rage." Frustration is an anger emotion, too.

Response: Identify the rule or boundary that has been broken. Articulate it out loud to yourself.

Sometimes when you articulate the rule, you'll hear yourself say it (a rule like "people should care as much as me") and think "*Ha!* I'm an idiot." Some rules are left over from when we were little kids, like "everybody has to be nice to me." That's a rule a four-year-old has, but you might still be carrying it around.

If you say the rule out loud to yourself and realize it's a bit silly, your anger should dissolve at this point. (If not, go to step 2.)

Identify whether the person was aware of the rule or boundary they violated. Did they know they were breaking your rule?

Often we have a framework of rules that people don't know about consciously. The other day I felt annoyed because I bought some people lunch and they didn't say thank you while they were eating (but they did thank me when we left). I have a rule in my own mind that it's polite to say thank you specifically during the meal, but they didn't know that.

So ask yourself: Did this person ever agree to play by that rule?

3. If they knew about the violation, communicate with them about it and enact an appropriate consequence.

An appropriate consequence is any kind of remedy for the situation that matches the intensity of the violation. There might be something they can do to clean up or fix the problem they caused. You might just require an apology. Sometimes the consequence is simply that they have to listen to you rant about how upset you are for long enough until you feel better!

4. If they didn't know about the violation, *and* it's not unreasonable or childish (see step 1), communicate the boundary and ask if they can honor it in the future.

If they say yes, it's happy days. By this point in the process your anger should be satisfied.

If they say no, you might just have to take your ball and go home. If you play with people who don't share the same rules, the game is hard to play and painful.

SADNESS

Message: "I have lost something or am losing something."

Sadness highlights any type of loss. It could be the loss of opportunity, something material, power, control, or love. Feeling overwhelmed also belongs on the sadness spectrum; it indicates a loss of control and a fear that you'll miss or lose something because you have too much to handle. FOMO is a sadness reaction. The intensity of the sadness will be in proportion to the scope of the loss.

Spectrum: From "Meh—a little bit miffed" to "irreconcilable grief." Overwhelm and powerlessness sit here, too.

Note: You have to know which time zone your sadness is rocking. Are you sad about losing something from your past, your present, or your future?

Women are particularly skilled at projecting into the future.

This is a good thing from an evolutionary perspective; in general, women are more dexterous than men at mapping future outcomes, with consideration for things like resource management and social dynamics. This acuity for mapping the future of social connections also means that we get into deep feelings really quickly. So we go on a date with someone and they never call us again and that makes us really sad. The time we actually spent with them was only a few hours, but (forgive the stereotype) it results in long nights on the couch with ice cream, crying.

(Continued)

(Continued)

It's not that we're sad over the loss of the time spent on that one date; we're sad because we projected a whole future with that person. We're grieving the loss of an imagined future, and it stings.

Response: Identify what you're losing or have lost. Identify if the loss is from the past, present, or future. Identify also whether it's a real or imagined loss.

"My dog died" should provoke a different flavor of sadness than "I didn't win the lotto." If you identify that you're grieving an irrational future projection, the sadness should go away.

But often sadness is to do with something very real. If that's the case, go to step 2.

If the emotion is still there, you've got to respond. Here are some ways to deal with sadness:

Balanced perception: Sadness comes from a perceived loss. Could you perceive the situation in terms of gain instead? Identify the things you're gaining out of these events that you can't enjoy or acknowledge because your focus is taken up with sadness. It might be a new stage of a relationship, an unexpected opportunity, a lesson learned, or some new insight into yourself/life/others.

Prioritization: In the middle of your sadness, what's the most important thing to focus on right now?

For example, a woman who's lost her husband might get through by focusing on her children or her purpose. Identifying the most important priority helps you respond to the situation in a productive way. Once you've decided what to focus on, you can build a series of little steps. As you start to tick them off, you gain momentum and a sense of control; eventually this will help the sadness move away. (I'm not making light of this—with something really profound, like the loss of a loved one, overwhelming sadness will take a long time to go away. You just start by getting through each day and eventually you have a new life and the sadness no longer dominates.)

Permission: Often you get to a point where you can give yourself permission to let the sadness go. Many cultures have good frameworks for dealing with grief that give people a set amount of time to wallow in the mess before they have to pull themselves together and leave the sadness behind. (Unfortunately that's not true in Australian, English, and American cultures—we're terrible at this.) If you don't already have a framework in place for processing grief and loss, maybe you can create a meaningful ritual of your own with a timeframe and permission to let the sadness go.

FEAR

Message: "Be prepared."

Fear is a Boy Scout. "Be prepared" is the Boy Scout motto.

I like to think of my fear as my own personal Boy Scout, who is *vigilantly prepared for any situation*. He lives in my brain and constantly assesses my environment. What's going to go wrong? What are the threats? The message is the same no matter where your fear is on the spectrum, but the intensity of the emotion is in proportion to how much you need to be prepared.

Spectrum: "Caution, concern, and nervousness" to "paralyzing terror." (Phobias sit at this end of the spectrum.)

Response: Identify the perceived threat. Articulate it to yourself.

Sometimes you realize that it is not going to happen, and the fear will disappear.

Identify whether the fear is real or imagined.

If it's an imaginary fear, acknowledging that it's not real might be enough to dissolve the fear.

If it's a real fear, or your brain tells you it's a real fear, you need to respond.

For example, if someone is running at me with a weapon, I have real fear. I need to respond by running or fighting.

(Continued)

(Continued)

If I'm walking down a dark alley and I hear a noise, I might imagine that somebody is going to run at me and attack me. This is an imaginary fear, so I ask myself how likely the threat is to manifest. If it doesn't seem that likely, the fear might dissolve or it might only require a small response to manage the fear. I get my phone out and hold it in my hand, and I feel safe. If my brain tells me this threat is mega likely to occur, it nudges the realm of being a real fear. I might kick my high heels off, turn and run.

A note on anxiety: Anticipating the future is an activity that all our brains are doing, for some of us more loudly/persistently than others.

If you're a person who is constantly projecting into the future and processing all the things you don't want to happen, anxiety is an appropriate emotional response. It's an action of your brain that you might not be able to control. I like to help people reframe statements like "I have anxiety" or "I'm an anxious person" into "I do anxiety." It's just a thing your brain does, not a thing you have. Because when you have it, it has you.

If it's something your brain does, you get more power by being separate from your brain that is doing the projecting. The purpose of this is to give you more power. Anxiety plus power is way better than anxiety alone.

HURT

Message: "An expectation hasn't been met."

Spectrum: "A little bit let down" to "heartbreaking devastation." Heartbreak and disappointment are hurt emotions.

Response: Identify the expectation and articulate it.

With anger, a line has been crossed; with hurt, the line has not been met. But there's still a line, and the line is of our own making. Say your expectation out loud and decide whether it's reasonable and important or not. (If not, the hurt should stop here.)

If the hurt is still there, the expectation matters. Go to step 2.

Identify whether the person knew about the expectation they didn't meet.

If you hold to an expectation that you haven't communicated, it follows that you can't reasonably be hurt when somebody doesn't meet it.

If the person knew about your expectation, and it's an important reasonable expectation, go and communicate about it. Ask them if they can honor your expectation in future.

If they say yes, the relationship and the hurt should be healed.

If they say no, you have an opportunity to ask yourself whether the relationship is more important than your expectation or not. I don't recommend that people compromise on their personal rules and boundaries (if the boundaries are important and reasonable). But I do recommend that people be flexible with expectations. It's up to you whether the relationship is worth more than the expectation, and whether you can be satisfied in it even if your expectations aren't met.

GUILT

Message: "I have violated one of my own standards, a code of ethics or a moral framework."

Spectrum: "Impertinence" to "devastating self-hatred."

Feeling impertinent is what we get from a little violation that probably doesn't have any huge consequences, like eating a second piece of chocolate cake or making someone else the object of a friendly joke.

Humans do a lot to avoid guilt; it's a very healthy evolutionary feature. Sociopaths and narcissists don't have a normal guilt reaction, and if everyone was like that, society wouldn't work. Thank fuck most of us not only have a very strong guilt reaction, but that for the majority of us our guilt lives in the

(Continued)

(Continued)

future time zone. We think about doing something and our conscience tells us no—we feel bad just thinking about it. Guilt is a brilliant guidance system!

It's worth noting that if you feel guilty about something that hasn't happened yet, this means you're probably considering doing it.

Response: Guilt about a potential future action tells you not to do it. If you do go through with it, you'll have real guilt—guilt about the past. This response is for guilt about a past action.

Identify the personal standard, moral, or ethic that you breached.

Identify whether that standard was realistic, practical, and relevant.

Context is important. Should a soldier feel guilty about the things he did in war, or was it contextually appropriate? If the standard you're holding yourself to was unreasonable in the context, you can let it go.

Give yourself a break.

Guilt is incredibly powerful, biologically. If your violation was real, you can't shake the feeling until you take some action.

Acknowledge that you've violated a principle—to yourself and/or to the person you've wronged.

Evaluate what you think is the appropriate recourse or correction, if there is any.

Sometimes you can't make amends because somebody has died or disappeared from your life. But the guilt from this situation can guide your future behavior. I can't ever apologize to my grandmother for the things I feel I should have done or said before she died, but I can make sure that when I interact with other elderly people I show them massive appreciation and listen a lot.

Assess whether the principle you violated is important enough that you want to keep in the future.

If you still want to hold to the principle, commit to it for the future. Make a promise to yourself or another person. Rehearse in your mind how you would handle the situation differently next time.

Once you've made this commitment, the majority of the intense guilt feeling should go away.

If it persists, there might be other guilt to deal with. If you can't identify anything else, and the feeling turns into wallowing, it's probably become shame. You've identified with the bad thing you did and decided that you're now a bad person.

SHAME

Message: "I am bad."

Spectrum: "I did a bad thing so I'm a bad person" to "unrelenting self-loathing."

Guilt says "I did something bad"; shame says "I *am* bad." It's an identity issue. The only way to respond properly to shame as an identity issue is with therapy. I highly recommend professional coaching with a practitioner of Neurolinguistic Programming who does TimeLine Therapy® for this.

In the meantime, here's the response you can try yourself:

Response: Acknowledge that you're experiencing shame, which means you're not dealing with the real world.

What I mean by this is that shame is an internal issue. It's an issue of your own interpretation, which is not necessarily related to reality.

Of course, you can justify its reality by saying, "but I did all those bad things." If that's true—if you've really done bad things—the way to deal with them is by using the guilt process above. If you've processed and made amends, but you still feel shame, you're hung up on something internal.

Identify as many "bad things" as possible and do the guilt process on each of them.

This helps weed out reality from your interpretation. Once you've dealt with the reality of anything you've actually done, you'll notice if you still feel shame.

(Continued)

(*Continued*)

Pick one thing that you could do that would be evidence of being a good person.

It doesn't matter if it's a big or small thing. Pick something good you can do and go do it. Allow yourself to enjoy the pleasure of having done it.

If you're dealing with residual feelings of shame that you can't shake—if you still think you're a bad person even after you've dealt with the "bad" things you've done and started doing "good person" things—I recommend that you seek help for dealing with your shame.

ABOUT YOU

As you read through all of the emotional processes above, notice how you react to each one. Which one do you judge? Which one seems self-indulgent or lazy? Which one seems smart or justified? Which one do I gloss over and try to ignore?

All of that is interesting feedback on your own emotional world.

Now try it out: Pick something from your past that's still emotionally charged up. Do the exercise until you're done with the emotion. If you get stuck—time for some therapy!

PHYSICAL

Coaching Exercise: Find Your Physical Thing

WITH EMILY

I see exercise as a need meter. Everybody's needs are different. Some people (like Tamara) don't need to exercise a lot to feel healthy but instead live an active life and eat well. If that's you, cool! Blend your exercise and make it a walk to the jazz festival with the kids! Double tick.

But you might want to look a certain way, feel a certain way or possess certain capabilities. For example, for myself:

I want to feel good, physically and emotionally.

I want to feel physically capable—I want to know that I can pick up the couch and move it by myself. (It bothers me that I can't do pull-ups, because what if I were stuck on the side of a building and I needed that ability?!)

I want to be able to learn new things, and I know there's a certain amount of cardiovascular activity needed for the brain to function properly—damnit!

I have neck nerve damage, so if I go more than three weeks without doing corrective exercises, my arm stops working properly and things don't go well—pain evasion.

Your personal needs and desires will determine your physical goals.

Humans naturally resist exercise, to conserve energy. The more needs you can meet with a particular activity, the less likely you are to resist. The exercises you stick with consistently will be the ones that answer multiple desires and best match your values.

For example, I have the social, intellectual, and spiritual need to do a team sport. It keeps me learning new skills and gives me a strong sense of belonging. I also wanted to spend more time with my sister, and joining a team together was a way to do that. So playing a sport ticks a lot of boxes for me. It's way easier to comply with an exercise routine when there's a "need stack."

Another thing to consider is what your favorite emotional "flavor" is. I'm an anger person; I tend to get angry before I feel anything else. I play hockey, which is a really aggressive sport. It's a healthy place for me to express normal, primal emotions in a safe environment with other adults who have agreed to do the same thing. If you're a sadness person, you might like an introspective activity like yoga. If you feel a lot of shame, something inhibition-lowering like dance might help you shed the shame and increase your level of self-love.

(Continued)

(Continued)

One great example comes from a woman I know who is really motivated by socializing, laughter, fun, and connection—those are some of her main values. On the flipside, her favorite emotional flavor is anxiety. So she didn't want to play a team sport, or anything where she felt like she had to perform. But she still wanted connection, community, and fun. She joined a local community hula hooping group! She's not letting anybody down, there's no performance pressure, but she still feels connected and feels really good about herself.

So here's the exercise:

1. Revisit your list of values that you made in Chapter 5.
2. Write a list of physical activities you've got a curiosity for. (The list of curiosities from Chapter 9 of this book might help.)
3. Start to draw lines between which activities meet which values. Identify the activities that meet the most needs, and match your favorite emotional flavor. We covered this in the "Emotional" exercise earlier.

Now pick something and try it! Everyone has a different thing. Persevere until you find yours, and exercise will never be a chore.

NOTES

1. M. Mackenzie, "Why CEOs Need to Talk About Mental Health," *Forbes,* May 15, 2018, https://www.forbes.com/sites/macaelamackenzie/2018/05/15/mental-health-awareness-month-why-ceos-need-to-talk-about-mental-health/#12a6110553c2. The article was referencing M. Freeman et al., "Are Entrepreneurs Touched With Fire?," prepublication manuscript, April 17, 2015, http://www.michaelafreemanmd.com/Research_files/Are-Entrepreneurs-Touched-with-0Fire-(pre-pub-n)-4-17-15.pdf.
2. T. Ferriss, "Some Practical Thoughts on Suicide," *Tim Ferriss Blog,* May 6, 2015, https://tim.blog/2015/05/06/how-to-commit-suicide.

CHAPTER 9

Breaking Out of Your Bubble

How to keep growing into the person you want to be

When it comes to the area of your "Self," there's one more thing I want to talk about.

First I want you to feel stable because your pie has all the right pieces, I want you to be doing all the preventative work to protect your mental health, and I want your soul to be filled. But when all those things are in place, you probably still won't be satisfied. There's something else that high-performing women need in their personal pie.

I'm talking about growth and learning. When you stop learning, you stop living. I love learning. There has to be room in my pie for that. When I haven't been to any learning events for a while I'm not myself.

Learning doesn't have to mean studying from books: The aim is to get wiser. I don't think that people write down on their bucket list "I want to be a wise old man" (or woman), but if you're a career-driven type or an entrepreneur you'll have a curious mind. So learning is always important, but you need to define learning; it doesn't always mean reading a book or studying a degree or going to a Tony Robbins seminar.

Here's how I think of it:

Learning is anything that leads you toward the person that you want to be.

Everybody's version of this type of learning will look different, so I'm not going to tell you exactly how to pursue it. I only have a couple of recommendations for maximizing your learning and staying curious.

GET OUT OF YOUR BUBBLE

Most of us tend to learn more about the things we're really good at, and sometimes we forget there are other things in the world we could be learning about. Learning isn't just about getting better at one thing!

My first recommendation is to learn more about the things that the voices in your head tell you you're bad at. If you and your partner want to be better parents, go figure that out. If you're underconfident in one area of your career, focus on the thing that's holding you back. There are some things you're never going to be good at and that's fine, but don't just bury those things; at least look at them from time to time. Don't fall into the trap of only learning more about the things you already know. It feels good but it won't take you anywhere new.

My second recommendation is to be open to experiencing things you wouldn't normally like or choose. In other words, get out of your bubble. This is one of the reasons I love Entrepreneur's Organization and Young Presidents' Organization, because we all take turns to pick things we do. Each person in my forum is in charge of planning one forum retreat and we all have to do what they plan. The best things are always the things that make me go, "I do not want to do that, not in a million years have I ever wanted to do that." I don't have a choice, because it's somebody else's bucket list item. I always walk away from a new experience going, "Wow, I can't believe I just did that! That was so fucking cool!"

The Pattern Interrupt

My friend Sue-Ellen is amazing at getting out of her bubble. She calls it the pattern interrupt:

> There was a time when I was going through an extremely challenging time, and I was finding it difficult to break out of it and take back my control of the situation. I decided that what I needed was a pattern interrupt, and the best kind of interrupt is a physical one!
>
> I'm quite afraid of heights. I've never had it on my bucket list to do any sort of extreme activity, so

this something extreme was going to be the perfect interrupt! I wrote down on a piece of paper all the baggage I wanted to let go of, and I jumped off the second-highest bungee in the world, letting go of the piece of paper and my mindset around those challenges on the way down. It was an incredibly freeing activity that marked a line in the sand for me to see my challenges as opportunities and move forward in a positive and proactive way. It actually worked!

A few years later I found myself in a position where I felt I was holding back in business. I usually don't have any aversion to risk, but I was feeling fear in my decision making, which was slowing me down. So I decided it was time for another pattern interrupt and to address fear in a physical way. I got up one morning and jumped out of a plane. I'd never wanted to do that, no desire, and I am more than happy to never do it again! That afternoon I picked my three boys up from school, and they asked me how was my day. I said "Great, I jumped out of a plane this morning." They weren't expecting that!

It's all about pushing my mental boundaries in an extreme way to push past my blocks. I love the pattern interrupt to shake it up when I need it!

—Sue-Ellen (Sel) Watts
Founder, wattsnextpx, wattsnext,
Your Secret Sauce, and zzoota
Vlogger of The Unconventional Life,
https://www.youtube.com/channel/
UCFhMSaKj43f0EXM-4b_H1DA

GROW YOUR RING SIZE

When a tree is cut in half and you look at it, the rings in the trunk tell the story of its life. Each ring shows a different stage of its development. In stages where there was drought and struggle, the rings will be thinner because they didn't have much to feed on. The wider rings reflect the times when the tree had access to more water and resources. The tree will expand when there's abundance and take what it can without apologies. And when there's a drought it doesn't apologize, either; it just shrinks and regathers and gets ready to grow again. Life's the same.

If you're a tree and somebody cuts you in half, what will your rings say about you? On average, I've changed careers every five years. So it's obvious I don't want to be a Paperbark, which you cut in half and there's no rings. There's not much substance to a Paperbark; it's all fluff. No, I want to be a wise old tree with heaps of rings, big ones.

Think about the size of the rings you want to grow. Yes, sometimes you're going to see a lot of change naturally because of abundance and things coming easily. But you can also push for change, and make the size of your rings bigger on purpose.

This is something Richard Branson taught me about growth and change. Imagine that you're standing in the middle of your current ring. Now imagine that you're going to draw a slightly larger ring outside of the one you're standing in. That's your new life. Whatever decision, change, or learning you're doing right now, it's going to expand your life and add a new ring outside of the one you're standing in now.

Most people can comfortably cope with a ring that's about 10% bigger than the one they're in. If the degree of change is more than 10%, you're going to get uncomfortable. That's why everyone gets so depressed coming down from the Christmas season: We've all spent more than 10% over our usual budget, our diet has been more than 10% different than usual and we've probably spent more than 10% of our time on holiday-related things that we don't normally do. Even if it's enjoyable, it's stressful.

That's "average" people—the rate of change they can cope with is 10%. But if you're reading this book, you're probably not average. You've probably got more of an entrepreneurial mindset, and entrepreneurs tend to draw bigger circles of change, up to about 30%.

So think about it: How big are the rings you like to draw? Is it 10% growth, 90% growth, or something in between? Wherever you are now, could you draw a bigger ring? Even if you just allow yourself 1% more change than you're normally comfortable with, you're growing. You're on the way to being a bigger, wiser tree.

When I take the step into the 30% larger ring I just drew for myself, the doubt sets in. I'm a little fish again, I'm surrounded by inspirational people playing a much bigger game, and I'm squirming ... with a massive grin on my face!

I've drawn a few rings over the past two decades, enough to know that challenge serves me. I acknowledge and respect these feelings and become a sponge; I'm open to learning, okay with asking what seem like silly questions and confident that I will soon fill that area, enjoy it for a while, and then grab another piece of chalk and start drawing circles again.

Don't expect everyone (or anyone) to get it. Even the people closest to me, including my own parents, ask me repeatedly, "When will you ever be happy and content?" For me it's the journey that makes me passionate about life and connects me with the most inspirational humans on the planet. It provides a role model to my kids that doesn't involve one career or one model to live life and shows there are many ways to be happy.

Draw bigger circles, don't expect people to get it, and be unapologetic.

UNDERSTAND YOUR LEARNING STYLE

Everyone's got a different way of learning stuff. You need to understand your own style of development. Some people ask questions, some people seek facts, some people research, some people learn from experience.

I'm more of an auditory learner than a reader. During the 10 years that I was reading business books I learned less than in the two years I've been in EO and YPO. I love hearing people share their experience, not telling me what to do (I hate being told!) and I'm not into textbooks. If I'm excited and somebody's talking to me about a topic I'm interested in, I can absorb that better and even regurgitate it to somebody else later. It sticks. Find the learning channel that makes your brain a sponge.

I call my style "do the opposite." Whatever everyone else is doing, I do the opposite. In business and in life. (Heck, I'm even left-handed!) When I was 30 everyone was getting married; I questioned my first marriage and got divorced. When other marketing agencies were chasing big names like Coca-Cola, I thought, What are the accounts they aren't chasing that pay just as much money for their marketing? And I chased those instead. When I met Florian I thought, I'll have children with this man first, as that's a bigger commitment we agreed on together, and then if we haven't killed each other we'll get married. Then he stayed at home with the babies and I was back on emails two days after giving birth. Now I'm starting to explore venture capital, which has such a bad image, but that's because everyone else is doing it a certain way. I want to do it *my* way. The opposite.

I think when you do the opposite is when you stumble on some pretty cool stuff, but that's hard. Sometimes I wish I could be satisfied like everybody else. Why can't I be happy with a marketing agency that turns over 1.3 million dollars a year? Why can't I invest in businesses "normally," by giving money and taking equity?

But that's not me. What other people perceive as the rules, I see as guidelines to how things have been done before. I don't accept things as they are. I see them as I want them to be: fair and an opportunity to reinvent the norm. That's where the growth happens.

My friend Holly said to me once, "Everyone says 'I'm a peg, where's my hole? Where do I fit?' But when there's no hole, you just make a hole."

That sounds like me.

In the previous chapter we covered how to stay stable and healthy. You probably need to have a certain baseline before you can invest energy in your growth, so if you need to do that work first, go back to Chapter 8.

If you're ready to grow, here's the next exercise and the next section for your bucket list. Do the exercise first, then let that inspire the next lot of items on your list!

INTELLECTUAL

Coaching Exercise: Write a List of Curiosities

WITH EMILY

A "curiosity" is anything you're interested in. Something that keeps drawing your attention or calling your name, even if you don't know why.

There are no rules around curiosity. You might be resistant to pursuing something interesting because you can't see how to turn it into a business, or it doesn't seem to fit with your image of yourself. What if you stopped judging it and just surrendered to the fact that you're curious about it?

Stop worrying for a moment about what other people think, or your feeling that this curiosity might be frivolous or unproductive. This is something inside you that you don't get to control! This curiosity is innate to you as a unique individual.

You'll never know what a curiosity will bring into your life. It's never just about learning the thing itself.

So write your list of curiosities, and pick one to learn more about. Block out a chunk of time in your diary when you're committed to doing that.

Humans are insatiable when it comes to curiosity. Allow yourself to occupy that space in your mind where curiosity gets ramped up. Once it gets strong enough, it will override any excuses and circumstances.

For example: Here's a list a client shared with me.

Photography

Art

Bridge

Chess

Gardening/Growing my own produce

Backyard chickens

Psychology

Fermented foods

Novels

Hula hooping

Swimming

Yoga

The lady who shared the list above is married, runs a household, is a surgical nurse, and had a five-week-old baby when she wrote the list. But she committed to picking one curiosity to follow up, and found an outdoor hula hooping class. Once she started going, all those external pressures disappeared into her desire to keep following this curiosity.

Building Your Bucket List: Learning and Growth

This part of your bucket list is for items around self-development, hobbies, curiosities, and learning.

Take a few minutes now to consult your list of curiosities, think about your learning style, and consider how far you'd like to stretch your rings of change. Now write a list of things to learn or ways you'd like to grow.

Examples to get you started:

Learn a musical instrument.

Find a career mentor.

Take a wine appreciation course.

Attend a personal growth seminar once a quarter.

Read a book on an area I want to work on.

Get a master's degree.

Develop a personal characteristic.

Speak another language fluently.

Travel to a country I've never been to before.

MY BUCKET LIST: THINGS TO DO FOR MY GROWTH

1. _____
2. _____
3. _____
4. _____
5. _____
6. _____
7. _____
8. _____
9. _____
10. _____

CHAPTER **10**

Choose Your Own Adventure

How to make career moves that match your values

I was born into a third-generation mining family. My role models weren't business owners; my dad has had the same job since he was 17. To this day, my mother has never driven a car. She was a 100% stay-at-home mom. But she was very motivational. She told us we could be anything, which was great.

Mining towns are very sporting orientated, very male oriented. Nearly every guy got a job in the mines and nearly every girl got married. I was different; I was artistic. I wanted a challenge, and high school wasn't challenging. It was horrible and I hated every minute of it. I spent a lot of time writing music and drawing. That was my outlet.

My father let me pick one subject at school and he picked the rest. He picked Maths 1, Maths 2, Physics, and Chemistry ... I picked Art. I graduated school with a pretty good score, enough to get in to university and study Law. My dad was horrified when I said I was going to study Art. He said art was a hobby, not a business.

College felt like high school: not much of a challenge. So I decided to do a minor in marketing on top of my major in visual art. I graduated early, when I was 19, and moved to Australia's Gold Coast for my first job at a marketing agency.

I figured out pretty quickly that it wasn't my scene—all egos and pool tables. I loved the work, though, so I decided to go out on my own and pick clients that I believed in. I was never one of those marketers who can sell ice to Eskimos. I can't do marketing for things I'm not passionate about.

I grew my agency, Mitara, to be one of the leading marketing agencies in Australia. At the same time I kept writing music and then got signed to a record label. I got married. I was doing songwriting tours, four to seven weeks at a time. I released my own album when I was 24, and two of the songs reached #2 on the Indie charts in Australia. I toured Japan with my band. I got divorced. I met Florian in London; six months later he was living in Australia with me. Six months after that I was pregnant.

I had my eldest daughter and went back to work less than one month later, while working from my laptop in between. My agency was turning over more than a million dollars a year, but I was stuck in more ways than one: I was tied to it all the time because all my clients wanted to deal directly with me, so I couldn't scale it.

I had our second daughter. I discovered sweat equity, and took equity in a food company even though I didn't know anything about food. I grew it to a 10-million-dollar turnover in two years, then realized I wouldn't enjoy the things I'd need to do to stay with it through the next phase of growth. I took equity in an indie haircare company.

By the time this book is published, I'll be doing something new. I think we can count on that.

WORK AS A JOURNEY, NOT A LADDER

> My stepdad told me: "Your instability is going to look really bad on your resume." I've never had a resume one day in my entire life! If it takes me three years to solve this problem and then I solve the next one in two years, that's not resume instability. That's efficiency!
>
> —Jeff Hoffman

"Job security," "career stability," "corporate ladder" ... these terms have a lot less weight than they used to, especially in a world that no longer honors a 40-year career.

I hear business owners talking up the fact that their retention rate on their staff is great—well, is high retention necessarily a good thing? The average attention span isn't good these days. I'd rather align with people's attention spans and energy levels. If I know somebody is going to get bored after two years, fine. If I can have them for those two years, that's great.

Why pigeonhole people into one career? This mindset starts at school. *When I grow up I'm going to be a fireman.* We need a shift away from that old conversation, and it starts with our kids!

Take my two girls. When my youngest was in preschool, they made all the kids write what they were going to be when they grew up on a sign and hold it up. She came home protesting, "Mom, I had to pick just *one*. Why?"

My older daughter was the opposite. She was like, "Mom, my sister keeps changing her mind. One week she wants to be a doctor, the next week she wants to be an artist, then she wants to own businesses." I said, "Does she keep changing her mind, or does she want to do all of those things?"

The youngest said she wanted to do *all* of them. "Great," I said, "that's your first three careers. I wonder what else you'll do."

When people ask you what do you do, how do you want to answer?

Think about this for a minute. What would you like to say? This isn't necessarily what you currently say, but what would your dream answer be? And if it's not what you're doing right now, how can you get there?

I'm an entrepreneur. I could never call myself that when people asked, not until I achieved my definition of what a true entrepreneur is. Mine is to build a profitable business and sell it. Your definition may be different. The thing about the word *entrepreneur* is that it covers a lot; it doesn't put me in a box or say that I can only do one thing. So it suits me in that way.

Your answer to the question "what do you do?" can be as simple or as complex as you want it to be. It might not be one job title, or even a job that exists. You might want to create something for yourself. Whatever it is, own it.

The chapters of your career are like the chapters of your life. What you liked in your twenties you might not like in your thirties. What you liked in your thirties might not appeal to you in your forties. So why do we expect one career to see us through? If you're going to stay committed to a career it needs to evolve with you, or you need to evolve out of it. Either way, give yourself permission to evolve.

My friend Dan on choosing your own adventure

I had a real estate business in Australia for 13 years. My business was in the supermarket industry and we started doing commercial property around that. I moved to the States three years ago because I burned myself out and wanted to do something fresh and creative.

I moved to LA, did a Masters in Spiritual Psychology and started making art as a result of that. I started painting and then did a live show where basically I took my clothes off and covered myself in paint. Just a fun, totally creative, off-the-wall experience.

I'm just about to start something new again. The three years has given me a bit of a refresh. I'll keep creating art on the side for sure, and at the moment I'm working in a startup that does tax incentives for TV commercials.

I still remember the day that I met Tam. It was kind of like love at first sight. She's really free-spirited. She is achievement-focused, but she does it in this kind of casual way. She's a big believer in coaching and she has never allowed her own thoughts to hold her back. Some people will see something and say, "I could never do that." Tam is the type of person who sees something and says, "Wow, that'd be cool if I could do that."

Tamara has one of the most interesting lives of almost any person that I know: marketing person, rock star, songwriter—she's one of those people who is good at anything she turns her hand to.

—Daniel Bonney, entrepreneur and artist

CHOOSING YOUR OWN ADVENTURE

I get bored easily and I like learning. No surprise there. So I'll tell you a career secret of mine: I don't actually choose my next career move based on my past experience. I base it on my mentor's approach: life design. Define what you're passionate about right now, go research it as someone outside the industry, define the problem, find a solution, and go about fixing it.

Let's take building startups as an example. I love growing small businesses, so I went in search of a channel for that. I tried venture capital (which is the obvious way to do it) and thought *oh my God, this is so compliant. This is so not my thing.* Then I found sweat equity and it suited my style much better.

My first sweat equity project was a prepared-meals company. I'd never worked in the food industry before. But I think it's really good to go into an industry that you don't know anything about, because you've got an outside point of view. You don't know what you don't know; you just set it up to be a really good business as opposed to what's standard in the industry. I didn't know anything about food but I was ready to just figure it out.

I went to get a mentor, which is always the first thing I do when I need to find out about something new. They said that becoming a successful food manufacturer takes 10 years, and it's often something that carries on through generations of families. It requires a lot of trial and error and a lot of time. They told me a bit about it and I knew I wasn't interested (they lost me at "10 years"!)—but I owned a food company. So I thought, great, what's another way I can do it? I decided to shut down our kitchen and partner with a manufacturer to create the food, while I focused on the marketing.

Manufacturing wasn't the thing that excited me, so instead I created a sales and marketing business that was committed to people's wellness, operating within the food industry.

The other thing that didn't excite me was the margins. Food manufacturing typically returns about 5–10%; I'd come from a service-based industry where I was used to 30% margins.

And I decided that I wanted to scale a business to a stage where it was turning over 10 million dollars, which I hadn't been able to do with my marketing business.

So I had this list of key things that I wanted the business to achieve for me: 25% returns, turnover above 10 million dollars, me dealing with marketing rather than the food itself. I shaped the business to fit that mold and achieve those things; I didn't worry about the industry norms. That meant unwinding a lot of things that were in place because they were the "normal" way of doing things. I didn't care about "normal": instead, I asked, *Is this the best way to do this?*

If you can see a better way of doing things—for yourself or for the place you work—don't worry if it hasn't been done that way before. People follow the same old traditional pathways and wonder why they don't get different outcomes. If you want to see different results, you have to change the way you do things. So don't be afraid to start with your own career.

Most of us pick an industry or a career path based on our previous experience or interest, then try to find a role within that industry that works for us. Try it the other way around! Think about the skills you have and the way you like to work, and see if you can match that to an industry or role that will allow you to operate that way.

It's exactly the same if you're thinking of buying or starting a business. Instead of coming up with an idea and then trying to make it work, why don't you go out and research the market? Find out what the gaps are, find out what's trending, then go out and find a business that you can shape to fit that. You've got a much better chance of success that way.

Passion is important. If you get bored with what you're doing, you won't do it well. But often we focus too much on the industry or the job title and not enough on the type of work or daily activities we'll be doing. I'm just as happy marketing a food business (which I knew nothing about) as any other type of business, because I love the creative side of marketing and strategy and I'm passionate about wellness and *not* cooking. Once the food business grew big enough that I was tied to my desk as the CEO, I was suddenly ready to move on, because I personally need freedom and flexibility much more than I need that title. The idea of heading up a multimillion-dollar business sounds really good, but it doesn't actually make me happy.

We've all heard that it takes 10,000 hours to become an expert at something. That might be true, but reinventing your career does *not* mean you have to start over again from zero. I really like the way my mentor, Jeff Hoffman, talks about how easy it can be to train in something new and switch careers: As you go through your career, you create a toolbox of skills. When you want to change tracks, you can pick up your toolbox and take it to another job site.

Most businesses and industries have similar challenges: They're just dressed up as different products and services. Valuable skills—such as managing people, holding a role on a board, setting KPIs, and doing strategy, sales, and marketing—can be taken anywhere. Should you want to redesign your life, take your toolbox and go learn about a new industry. You won't be going in empty-handed.

People think that it might take them three or four years to transition into a new industry. I've found that I'm able to do it in a lot less time, because I take my toolbox and then all I have to do is learn about that sector. More importantly, I'm looking at the industry from the outside, not having a long history of working in it, and that's why I usually think of different ways to do things. Without the baggage of "We've always done it this way," I'll think of different ways to approach the problems that I want to solve in that sector.

So when you want to change things up and look at a new career, don't think of it as starting again. Yes, you'll need to get yourself across a new industry, learn about trends, competitors, and everything else, but you already start miles ahead when you turn up with your already-refined skills.

No more excuses for saying, "I studied X in college, therefore I will be in that industry or role for the rest of my career." If that role doesn't excite you anymore, doesn't fit your current stage in life and tick your requirements, then reinvest in your career. Redesign your life. I do it every seven years as my passions and interests change, and I want my business to provide me different things.

It doesn't matter what you've done before: Right now, where do your skills fit best? Which industry or role is going to give you what you want out of work? Pick something that needs what you have, and change the rules of the game to suit the way you want to play.

DEFINING YOUR SUCCESS—AND GETTING IT

Once you've picked your career (for now), you get to decide what success in that career space looks like for you. Don't just assume that all the normal markers of success (like a bigger paycheck, bigger office or better title) are going to work for you. Climbing the corporate ladder is one definition of success, but is it the definition of happiness?

As much as *CEO* means big money and a great title, it was not me, not my way. I still want to make big money, but I know now that being an in-office CEO isn't how I'll do it. Being the CEO means you have to be in the office nine to five, babysit everything, be accountable, do compliance and reporting, and all the things I hate. In professional jobs, the big corner office is the dream. But that's not my definition of success.

My definition of success includes a lot of flexibility—deal making, co-labs, empowering teams (not managing them), problem solving, creative communities and brands, redefining the client experience, and of course making profitable businesses that impact lives.

Don't be held back by what's "normal." I was getting botox last week and I started talking to the lady doing it; she asked me what I do. I never really know how to answer that so I told her about all my businesses and my whole approach of being flexible. She made the throwaway comment, "Oh that's not an option for me, because I'm a clinician."

I challenged her on it. I said, "If you're really valuable to this company I bet you'd be granted some flexibility. I don't have the time to park my car here and sit in the waiting room. It annoys me. I don't even want to be seen walking into these places! So you could figure out a way to come to me, or better yet, let me come to your house. Give me a glass of champagne, do four of us at once, all entrepreneurs. You could take the idea to your boss and tell them you've got a new business concept and you'd like their support! See what they say."

Don't trap yourself into thinking that you need to do a whole lot of study or start all over again if you want a more satisfying career. Come back to what you love and what activities you want to do every day. Maybe you can stay in the same industry but do a different role, or have the same role in a different business. I figured out that I love growing startups to a certain size, so when I get to a stage where "my work here is done" and it needs someone else to serve it, I can go back and start again with another one.

Lots of people quit their jobs and join small businesses because they don't want to be stuck in corporate; let me tell you, small business owners love people like you! We get to pick up somebody who's got amazing experience but just wants to join a small team and have a sea change. A friend of mine just employed a funds administrator who was previously managing 750 funds at once, and now he manages five. The company gets the benefit of his experience and he gets to pick up his kids from school every day. For him, that's success.

If you're completely overwhelmed by the idea of redefining your role or changing careers, I get it. A lot of people stay in jobs they hate because they feel like it's too big a risk to try and change. Maybe you've got kids you need to support. If you've got a partner, talk to them about it. There's a huge chance you can take turns supporting each other.

If your partner isn't supportive or if you're on your own, think about the amount of change you *could* manage, even if it's tiny. Remember the rings of change? Just try making a change that's within 10% of your current normal. Then see how far you can push it.

If you want to make effective changes and get to your version of success, you need to surround yourself with people who can get you there. Even if you have a partner who's backing you, and *especially* if you don't.

When I met my business partner in Gutsii (*another* wellness brand!), she was reinventing her life. Although she was recently divorced, she wasn't a victim; she made it her choice to walk away from a partner and a business. She was confident in her ability and skill set. Plus she had an amazing idea that was on-trend.

Now that we're business partners, she's traveled with me to America a couple of times, where we blended my close friends and high-level business network, and from that we've formed an amazing friendship. Oh, and did I mention she's moved to LA? What a wonderful life design, and none of that was on a vision board.

What she was great at doing was defining her values and aligning to a business partner with the same ethics and passions. She's open to learning and drawing herself big-ass circles, and signed up to enjoy the journey.

People say you're the average of the five people you spend the most time with. So pick your five carefully. Find people who'll encourage you and expand your thinking. Find your tribe.

CREATING YOUR VOCATION

I say "creating" your vocation rather than "finding" it, because you might create something for yourself that isn't already an existing role or conventional career path. *Finding* implies that there's a perfect career out there, and once you find it, it'll fit forever. I'm sure you know by now that I don't believe in that because your priorities will change and your career will have to evolve to keep up.

So I talk about *creating* your vocation: It's a process that's always evolving.

This evolution is always about figuring out your next move. To pick your next move, based on where you are now, ask yourself some questions:

What do I enjoy?

What are my priorities?

How do I want to spend my time?

What does the ideal work environment look like for me?

If your current position doesn't match up with your ideal, choose to focus your energy on not complaining about the situation. Look at the list of ideals you've made, and look for solutions to make it happen.

Ask your trusted friends for feedback. Ask your network about opportunities. Keep an open mind and be prepared to do something you'd never considered before. If it fits your skills and serves your priorities, it might be the perfect fit.

Before you make a big move, check in and make sure that it suits your values. Does it align with the things that are most important to you? Does it allow you to be the person that you want to be? Does it give you a good gut feeling?

If you understand your value set and what fills up your soul, you'll know what's right for you. If your job doesn't involve a little bit of something that fills up your soul every day, you've got a disconnect. Go back to Chapter 8 and check in with your pie. You'll know what to do.

Building Your Bucket List: Vocation

This is a list of things you want to do on the way to creating your ideal vocation. What kind of things embody your definition of career success? What kinds of small changes can you make to stretch your comfort zone and grow it bigger?

Maybe success in this area will be defined by things you *don't* do. It could be that you want to escape employment and

work for yourself, or retire by a certain age. Maybe you want the flexibility to put family above work, or pursue a passion project.
Examples to get you started:

Create a side business that generates a passive income.

Provide employment for 100 people.

Publish a book.

Mentor a young person in my industry.

Have the freedom to work remotely from anywhere in the world.

Host a podcast.

Win an industry award.

Create and deliver a workshop around my expertise.

Position myself to work part-time while I have kids.

MY BUCKET LIST: THINGS TO DO FOR MY CAREER ADVENTURE

1. _____
2. _____
3. _____
4. _____
5. _____
6. _____
7. _____
8. _____
9. _____
10. _____

CHAPTER 11

Work-Life Blend

How to ditch balance and get people on board with blending

Framing the issue of work-life balance—as if the two were dramatically opposed—practically ensures work will lose out. Who would ever choose work over life?[1]

—Sheryl Sandberg, COO of Facebook

In Chapter 10 I talked about choosing your own adventure and checking your career moves against your values. The dream is to create a career where your typical workday includes doing things that fill up your soul.

A lot of us see work as something we have to get through so that we can afford the money to spend on the nice things that make our life worth it. Or so that we deserve to reward ourselves with a glass of wine at the end of the week, or a massage or a vacation. Or as a way of earning awards and recognition, so that we feel like we've done something worthwhile with our lives. Work is a way of earning pleasure and proving ourselves.

But the idea that the work itself can fill up our soul? Unfortunately, not many of us are "lucky" enough to like our jobs. We often resign ourselves to the idea that work isn't pleasant; that's just the way life is. People are living for the weekend.

As usual, I think the opposite. Let me be really clear on this: **Work and life are not two different things**. My work is part of my life. It's actually one of my favorite parts of life.

If this isn't true in your life, how do you get there? When you read Chapter 10 you might have been thinking, "easier said than done." Well,

nothing worth having is ever easy. That's what this chapter is going to be about—making small changes, drawing bigger circles, and figuring out how to create a daily blend of work and everything else.

But first I want to deal with this "work-life balance" myth.

THE MYTH OF "WORK-LIFE BALANCE"

The pursuit of work-life balance seems to be mostly a female problem. I think women have been conditioned to feel ashamed of loving work. For some reason, work is seen as an intrusion on what's supposed to be our life—raising a family, looking after our home, and having enough "me time" as well.

I personally find that working on something satisfying can be great me time, but apparently that doesn't count. There's also the implication that being at home with your kids isn't work, which is a joke if you've ever raised children!

If we do have kids and a career, we're not supposed to love work too much in case it looks like we don't love our children enough. If you're a mother, you know how much you love your children. As if work could ever take away from that!

Love is like the universe; we don't know how big it is and where it ends. People treat it like you've only got a finite amount of love to give. That's bullshit. I don't split my love in half and give 50% to work and 50% to my kids. If you've got a passionate personality, you're going to be passionate about everything in your life. It's not an either/or situation.

In general, men have the opposite problem from women: Nobody judges them for loving their jobs, but lots of men feel like it's not okay to say they want to spend more time at home. A 2015 study found that many of the men interviewed were pretending to work more hours than they did, figuring out smart strategies to meet targets and pass as ideal workers while sneaking off to do the school run or even go skiing with their kids.[2] The men who openly voiced their dissatisfaction or proposed reduced work hours (including requesting the type of flexibility that was usually offered to women in the same organization) were typically met with harsh penalties and marginalization.[3]

That's ridiculous when you consider that the men who cut their hours back without asking still managed to do what was required of them at work; many of those guys were perceived as star players who worked harder than their coworkers. They were proof that blending works, but they did it under the radar because their bosses weren't on board.

FACT: WOMEN GET PREGNANT

Pregnancy and childbearing *do not* have to kill your career. When I was pregnant I was the most productive I've ever been. It really worked for me; I was on fire! You're not drinking alcohol and you have 30% more blood being pumped around your body and your brain. I've never felt greater.

My husband, Florian, parented our children full-time from the day we brought our first daughter home from the hospital. I'm talking 3 a.m. feedings and everything, so that I could sleep through the night and get up to focus on work in the morning. I already had a thriving business that I'd built up over the previous 10 years. It made sense for me to go back to it almost right away.

But I know my situation is really unusual. A lot of women don't have the great experience with pregnancy that I did, and even fewer women have a partner who cares for the kids full time.

I'll talk more about stay-at-home daddies in Chapter 14; maybe that's an option you'd like to explore for your family. But for the vast majority of heterosexual couples, having children will be more disruptive to the woman's career than to the man's. Even if Dad does decide to stay home with the kids and let Mom go back to work, most couples don't start this arrangement until the baby is several months or even years old.

Which means that if you want to have children, you'll have to navigate a period of your life where you step out of your job for weeks, months, or even a few years, then try to resume your career where you left off before babies. And then you've got all the practical challenges: how to function at work when you were up all night feeding, who does the school run, and the agony of abandoning your kid at the daycare centre while she's sobbing "Mommy, don't go to work!"

Here are a couple of typical solutions women have come up with for handling work during our child-rearing years.

WORK-LIFE BALANCE MYTH #1: "JUST WORK PART-TIME!"

> I thought success would be combining career and family
> successfully at the same time. I thought I could scale back
> to part-time, and I'd ramp back up as the kids grew ...
> [But my] industry offered few if any professional part-time
> positions.
>
> —An anonymous female respondent to a survey of
> Harvard Business School graduates[4]

The mainstream solution to finding a balance when you have kids is to go back to work part time. Great! There are *so many* fulfilling career opportunities for a woman who needs to leave at 2 p.m. every day to pick up her kids.

Of course, to compensate for the fact that we're mothers, a lot of us will end up accepting part-time pay for a full-time workload, doing unpaid overtime to push up our performance. It's like a huge apology for the fact that we have other priorities during these years of our lives.

Some women do survive and thrive in part-time jobs. Part-time hours and job sharing are legitimate options in plenty of workplaces. If that's you and you're fulfilled, that's fantastic.

If you're the breadwinner in your family, it's unlikely that part-time is a sustainable option for you. This is a book for ambitious, rising women. A lot of you will want to resume your career at a certain level, and it's hard to do that unless you're willing to throw yourself back into it full time. There are no part-time jobs for C-level executives. Women may find themselves accepting a job well below their experience and pay grade, just because they're not in a position to be as available as they'd need to be for the higher-level roles they aspired to do (or actually did) before they had kids.

And even if you could land a flexible, challenging part-time role in your chosen field, if your career is a major source of satisfaction for you, the part-time option will be ultimately frustrating. *You're allowed to love your work*. It's okay to choose to spend eight or more hours a day working on a project or running a business, if that's what makes you happy.

The key word here is *choose*: If you've got young children, you might still want to have a lot of freedom around when, where, and how you work. It's not as simple as getting a nanny and going back to your 80-hour-a-week corporate job.

Maybe you don't have young children or even a partner, but you'd still like a lot of flexibility around when, where and how you work. That's valid, too. I'm talking a lot about having babies in this chapter because that was my experience and it's the experience of a lot of women, but you don't have to have children to earn the right to demand freedom in your work life.

WORK-LIFE BALANCE MYTH #2: "JUST BE YOUR OWN BOSS!"

If you can't carry on your career without committing to full-time hours plus travel and overtime, what other options have you got?

For a lot of women, the answer is to start their own business. The myth tells us that being our own boss will offer flexibility and freedom.

The reality is that running a small business is hard. If you run an operation with fewer than 10 employees, it probably all depends on you. It takes time and strategy to break through to the point where your business doesn't depend on you being available and active all the time. In the meantime, your lifestyle suffers. You probably would have experienced more flexibility if you'd gone back to work.

When I joined Entrepreneur's Organization I was placed in a group of peers who had much larger businesses than I did. Yet they had plenty of time to take vacations, their offices weren't calling them anywhere near as much as mine did, and they were playing golf all the time. I compared my lifestyle to theirs and thought I was doing something wrong.

In fact, it wasn't that I was doing anything wrong, it's just that the business I had at the time relied on my name, my face, and my personal involvement. The brand was associated with me, and clients wanted to deal with me personally even though I had a team of people who could implement the strategies I developed. I felt stuck because the success of the business was dependent on me working in it all the time. I couldn't get away—plus if I sold it, it would come with "golden handcuffs" and that's never going to suit me, having been self-employed since I was 19.

I believed that a bigger business would mean I would become even more stuck. But the opposite is actually true. If you can grow your business past the point where you personally need to be there all the time, you can become more free of it.

Nothing about having your own business gives you flexibility. But if you persevere, being a business owner will give you options. You want to grow a reliable team underneath you so that the day-to-day operation of the business isn't dependent on you. Ultimately you want to transition from a goodwill business that depends on your involvement to an asset-based business that can be sold (if that's what you want to do—remember, you're giving yourself options!).

The bottom line is that if you want freedom you need to grow your business, not keep it small. If you're playing a small game based on a myth, you shouldn't be afraid to think bigger.

Selfishly, I'd love to see more women in YPO: To meet the membership criteria, members head up a business with an annual revenue of 10 million dollars (or an enterprise value of 20 million plus). The disparity between male and female members is concerning and women are just as capable of running businesses this size.

Don't let myths around what it means to run a big business get in the way—you have management teams, sometimes boards, CFOs, and of course an asset for your family. I have way more flexibility now than when I had a small business.

FINDING YOUR BLEND

In the Chapter 10 we talked about making big changes, even when your ideal situation feels way beyond your reach right now. Even if you can only make changes 10% at a time, you can start making career moves that align with your values and fill up your soul.

Then once you've created that career that matches your skills and values, I encourage you to tweak the way you approach your work on a day-to-day basis, so that all of the pieces of your pie get the attention they need consistently.

This is what some people call *work-life balance*. But you already know that I think work-life balance is bullshit. Instead, I call it *blending*.

I'll give you some examples of what that looks like in my own life. But basically, whenever you find yourself torn between two important things, try and find a way to do both or bring them together: like me at the conference, taking questions in the hotel pool with my kids splashing around.

Once you've started to define what a blended life looks like for you, communicate it to the people around you. Invite a colleague to have a work conversation at your place over afternoon drinks, or talk to your boss about flexible office hours. Invite people to join you in an experiment with blending.

This might feel really uncomfortable for you, but remember, you're always allowed to start small. Try and think of some things you could easily blend right away. Even one thing. Once you've started to blend in little ways, it gets easier, so start with small behavioral changes.

DEFINING THE BLEND

My basic rule of thumb when it comes to blending is this: Whenever you find yourself torn between two things, try and blend them.

Recently I took my oldest daughter with me on a work trip to the States. It's no different from a courier taking his kid on his rounds with him, or like the other day when a guy came to my house to mow my lawn and he'd brought his son along. (This was during school holidays.) The first thing out of his mouth was an apology; he promised that his son would be no trouble and that he'd help out with the lawn. I said, "No problem, but he doesn't have to help you—does he want to jump in our pool?"

We shouldn't be apologizing for having kids to look after! Or for bringing them along to interact in the adult world! Don't ever apologize for that. Own the fact that your children are important, and your personal concerns are important. Be unapologetic about it.

Let's say somebody wants to meet with you in the afternoon, but you're committed to doing school pickup that day: Why not invite them to come to the park to meet you while your kids play on the playground? Instead of apologizing for the inconvenience, think of it as a power play! If they want to talk to you, they have to come and fit in with your life. How powerful is that? And chances are, even if they don't say it to you, they'll be thinking *I wish I could do that*.

INVITING PEOPLE INTO THE BLEND

People are afraid of blending in case it looks unprofessional. Or, as women who are used to prioritizing everyone else's needs, sometimes we're not comfortable with blending because it feels too self-indulgent.

But when you start to blend, you give other people permission to blend too.

Share the concept of blending with other people. Just ask them, "Do you have work-life balance? Have you heard of blending? I'm trying to do it, and this is how it works." Then if they think it's a great idea, ask them, "How can we do it together?"

You might do it with a colleague at work. You might say *Hey, we meet every Friday morning for a coffee and to go over the action items for the next week. Why don't we instead have that conversation on Thursday night on the phone after the kids are in bed, then our Friday mornings will be free. Or you could come to my place at 4 p.m. every Friday and we can have the conversation over a glass of wine and a notepad. Bring your kids and they can swim in the pool while we talk*. Open your home to people. It doesn't matter where the conversation takes place—your boss shouldn't care—you're just having a meeting.

If you share the concept with your boss, you can point out that you're doing the same amount of work, but you're able to be more effective when it's blended with your personal life. You'll probably find that those blended meetings go an hour longer, and even if you're distracted by your kids you'll cover more ground. People are willing to work a bit longer and do a bit more when they've been given more.

One thing you can't do is say that you want to blend but you're not granting your team the same flexibility. You can't be a hypocrite. If you're going to blend, everybody around you gets to blend to some degree.

One of my employees has a husband who works one week on and one week off; he's at home one week and away at work the next. She shares his roster with me, and she also shares it with our suppliers so that they know when she's available to go to Sydney to check samples. She doesn't travel during the weeks that her husband is home because she values their time together as a family. (She could easily have set it up the other way and traveled during weeks that he *is* home, when he's there to take care of their kids. But she *doesn't* travel when he's home, because she values their relationship just as much as she values the children.)

She asked me once, "What will I tell the suppliers as to why I'm not available those weeks?" I told her to tell them the truth! You say *that's the week that I want to be at home with my husband and kids* and you leave it at that. I knew it'd come back to me (as her boss), and it did.

The suppliers wanted to know why they couldn't have her down there any week they wanted. I just told them, "She's not available to travel. If you have to get on a plane and come up here that week, you can do that." That valuable employee is only able to blend because she has me advocating for her. It's important that as the head of the family or the head of the business, you be the one to declare that everybody is going to blend.

If you're not the boss, you might be obliged to ask permission to blend. Remember, if you don't ask, you don't get. The worst that can happen is you get a "no." And you can at least filter the blend down to the people you're in charge of and be an advocate for others.

Remember the study I referred to earlier, about men who feel pressure to pretend to work more than they do? One of the teams in the study managed to create their own blending culture together:

> We kind of have a shared agreement as to what work–life balance is on our team. We basically work really closely with each other to make sure that we can all do that. A lot of us have young kids, and we've designed it so we can do that. We've really designed the whole business [unit] around having intellectual freedom, making a lot of money, [and] having work–life balance. It's pretty rare. And we don't get pushback from above because we are squaring that circle—from the managing partners—'cause we are one of the most successful parts of the company. Most of the partners have no idea our hours are that light.[5]

That's my dream workplace: a company where the people are free to manage their own priorities and take turns picking up the slack so that everybody can meet all their commitments. If you run a business, it's within your power to create a place like that. And whether you're the boss or not, you can start by modeling the blend to people around you, and inviting them to join in.

Lastly, let's inspire each other with ways we are blending. I have shared a few ways I blend, so I'd love to hear of your experiences. Jump on our social pages and share what's working and what's not, and let's support each other. No judgment, no opinions, just experience sharing that's authentic and real. We'll get there faster and stand as a constant reminder to each other why it's so important to persist and practice the art of blending.

Good Blending: Professional, Permission-Giving, and Powerful

If you're still worried that blending might be perceived as unprofessional or indulgent, check out this perspective from one of my (male) business partners:

As one of Tamara's business partners I have experienced how she "blends" work, family and community service.

While she's an unparalleled leader in social media and online marketing, she unashamedly outsources or off-shores repetitive activities so she can focus her efforts on the "high-impact, high-value" thinking she's respected for. All of Tamara's partners, clients and customers immediately know what her values are and that ethics comes first. Part of that includes her demonstrable process of continually "blending" all aspects of her life. Don't be surprised as she insists you include social responsibility and "giving" as a cost of goods! It is above the line, not below! Since Tamara ties all her efforts and renumeration to measurable outcomes, she "routinely" surpasses recognized business benchmarks—and frequently "passes" on work that is not a fit to her values, ethics and "blended" way of living.

Tamara does not have "work hours" and business can occur at any time. Given her extensive travelling across the globe, I have received a call from America that was 2:00 a.m. in Australia! On weekends I've often joined her handsome husband, and delightful daughters and friends for an afternoon of drinks, laughs and the odd business chat at her home, or mine!

Monte Huebsch, Content 2 Convert
(content2convert.com.au)

STARTING SMALL

If you're new to blending, it might feel hard to get started. But it's no different to developing any other habit: Start with small changes.

It might help if you talk about it as an experiment. "Hey, I'm trying this blending concept out for a little while, I'll see how I go." Just try your own version of it, so you can get a little bit of positive reinforcement.

Here's a great guiding principle: Don't put yourself or other people in a situation where they feel torn. I often want to be in two places at once—what do I with that? Is there a way to bring those two things together so that I can be present for both?

It doesn't have to be as clear-cut as bringing your family to work or inviting your colleagues to your home. There are lots of places you can use as middle ground. We tend to assume that working in a cafe is for people who are self-employed or working remotely online. It doesn't have to be that way. You're allowed to work there, too! You can easily do a work meeting after school in a cafe with your kids. The best way to entertain them is to give them a milkshake. So go for milkshakes and have your business conversation.

There's no reason to feel guilty or unprofessional for blending your business and personal lives. Men have always conducted business over whiskey and cigars; this is our way of doing it. Women are so gifted at relating to people, and we get to bring that authenticity into our business relationships.

We want our work life to blend into our real lives, to be something that's meaningful in the world outside of work. Otherwise what are we doing it for?

Building Your Bucket List: Work-life blend

Get creative and think about ways you can meaningfully combine work and life. What's something you've always wanted to do with your staff? How can you teach your kids to be entrepreneurial?

(Continued)

(Continued)

Examples to get you started:

Take each of my children with me on a special trip when I travel for work (one-on-one time).

Take my whole staff team on a weekend retreat with their partners and kids.

Set up my work life so that I can always be home for the kids' bedtime.

Help everyone on my team to write their own bucket list.

Once a year bring my partner to a work conference and extend it with a romantic weekend.

MY BUCKET LIST: THINGS TO DO FOR MY BLEND

1. _____
2. _____
3. _____
4. _____
5. _____
6. _____
7. _____
8. _____
9. _____
10. _____

NOTES

1. S. Sandberg, *Lean In: Women, Work and the Will to Lead* (New York: Alfred A. Knopf, 2013).

2. E. Reid, "Embracing, Passing, Revealing, and the Ideal Worker Image: How People Navigate Expected and Experienced Professional Identities," *Organization Science* 26, no. 4 (April 20, 2015), https://pubsonline.informs.org/doi/10.1287/orsc.2015.0975.

3. E. Reid, "Why Some Men Pretend to Work 80-Hour Weeks," *Harvard Business Review* (April 28, 2015), https://hbr.org/2015/04/why-some-men-pretend-to-work-80-hour-weeks.

4. Harvard Business School, "Life & Leadership After HBS: Findings from Harvard Business School's Alumni Survey on the experiences of its alumni across career, family, and life paths" (2015), www.hbs.edu/women50/docs/L_and_L_Survey_2Findings_12final.pdf.

5. Reid, "Why Some Men Pretend to Work 80 Hour Weeks."

CHAPTER 12

When Breadwinning Doesn't Feel Like "Winning"

How to cope with pressure and keep your financial promises

This is not a personal finance book. That's not my area of expertise, so I'm not going to give you a bunch of spreadsheets and rules for managing your money, and expect you to follow them. I don't expect you to handle your finances the same way that I do because I'm not a guru.

Your numbers will be different from the next person's numbers, and the numbers that *matter* to you will be different from the numbers that matter to other people. Some people just need to know that they're covering their living expenses; some people are trying to hit particular income goals to create options and freedom. Some people measure their worth by their total asset value and other people are happy if they've got plenty of cash this month. So I'm not going to give you a one-size-fits-all model for managing your money.

What I *am* going to talk about is what it's like to be a breadwinner and how that impacts your relationship with your partner and family. And I'll give you some very, *very* broad principles that I personally use to make decisions around money: how I communicate my expectations, keep my commitments, and define the numbers that matter to me.

WHEN BREADWINNING DOESN'T FEEL LIKE WINNING

I hate the term *breadwinner*. It assumes you're going to be winning all the time, when you're not. Why don't we called it "breadmaker"?

Sometimes it's brilliant and everybody wants bread. Other times, people are like, I'm gluten-free, I'm low-carb. Sometimes you're going to burn the loaf!

Men have been doing this breadwinning thing for centuries and it's really hard. Is it any wonder they work such long hours? When you're the primary earner you're under an incredible amount of pressure to provide.

I don't think you should look to your partner to understand the pressure you're under if they haven't experienced it themselves. Don't make them feel bad because they don't get it. (I can say this because I'm guilty of it.) They don't understand what it feels like to not be able to breathe over a work thing. They've got their own pressures.

Florian has told me that sometimes when I walk in the door at the end of a workday, I don't hear what the kids are saying. It can take me about 10 minutes to get into family mode because my brain's still at work. It's great that I live so close to my current office, but often my phone conversation from the car hasn't ended by the time I get home. So we made a deal that I'd end my calls before I walk in the door, even if it means waiting in the car. I can't drive into the garage because the kids hear it and know I'm home, so I sit in the car across the street. I wonder what the neighbors must think—my house is right there! It's because I made a promise to Florian that I would walk in the door, not on the phone, ready to be present. I'm caught up in what's happened at work, but that's not my family's problem.

It's not always that easy to switch off when you get home. When I feel like I can't breathe at work, like I don't have options, is when I can get disgruntled about my role in the family. It's not their problem, but if you're grumpy they're going to feel it anyway. If you've got a partner, keep communicating about how you feel and what you want to change. But don't expect them to fix it. When I expect Florian to understand and solve my work issues and he doesn't, I interpret it as him not caring. That doesn't help either of us.

I'm not convinced that I have great coping mechanisms for this, other than to be able to call my forum urgently and hear that everybody else has had the same experiences. You just need to find people who've been through it and survived it. Know that you're not alone, and get some ideas that might help you cope or get out of the situation.

So that's my top strategy for coping with the pressure of breadwinning: rather than looking to your partner to figure it all out for you, go to your network to help you solve the problem. Have moments with other breadwinners who can share when they're not winning.

The other coping strategy I have when I'm in a tight spot is to sit down and write out all the times in the past that I've pulled a rabbit out of my hat. If I list all those times when I came up with a magic solution, what are the patterns and trends across those moments? Where have I evolved and problem solved? After 20 years in business, I've got a breeding farm of rabbits. I can go to the rabbit store and get a solution.

The main thing is to have a plan, eat the elephant one bite at a time, and give it time. If you've got major dissatisfaction and stress around work and money, it's like a kind of grief. You want to get over it tomorrow, but you can't. It's a process.

Warren Rustand, one of our lecturers at the Entrepreneurs Masters Program in Boston, has a different approach. He doesn't buy into "stress." He believes that it's inevitable that things will go wrong. All you can do to prepare for this is know that you did your best at the time and then cope with the lessons and learnings that follow. He refers to stress as a waste of energy.

I'm looking forward to working on that part of myself to come closer to this model, because I believe this skill will not only help my mental health but also show up positively in my family. Warren is a shining example of this.

TALKING TO YOUR PARTNER ABOUT MONEY

We've all heard that financial issues are one of the most common reasons couples get divorced. So we need to get better about communicating about money!

The rise of female breadwinning has shaken up the roles we take financially, but maybe not in the way you'd expect. The old thing used to be that the man would be the breadwinner, but in many households he'd hand over his wages and the woman would run the finances. She'd have the checkbook, order the groceries, make sure all the bills got paid on time. But now that we're the breadwinners, do we hand over our money to our partners? I dare you to run that fucking survey! The answer would be "no."

So it's not a straightforward role reversal; we're all trying to figure this shit out as we go. Every couple is going to find their own way to share the money and the responsibility that goes with it. There are a few areas you might want to have a conversation about:

Asking for permission. Some couples need to get permission from each other before they spend anything. That's not the way I do it. I don't check the credit card statements or question what Florian spends. Sometimes I'll make a general comment like, "Hey babe, we talked about cutting back this month!" But I'm not looking at every purchase and adding things up.

As the breadwinner I don't ask Florian if I'm "allowed" to do something or buy something. But I do look to him for permission in the sense that I like to get his opinion on the things I want to do. I value it so much because he's got a helicopter view of my life and he's amazing; you couldn't ask for anyone less judgmental. He's always in my corner. He's my family. When you see each other like that, asking for permission sounds like, "Hey, I want to do this—do you think it's a good idea for us?" Not trying to find ways to get them to say yes to something and not punish you for it later. We don't play that game.

Taking risks. If you're in a partnership, the risks that you take financially matter to the other person. Some people are afraid of scaring their partner because they have very different risk profiles. But incompatibility isn't the main problem; not communicating about it is what causes the problem. You need to talk about the kinds of risks you're each comfortable taking and how you're going to involve each other in that. Risk profiles change and develop over time: what *Florian* may consider high-risk (not having been in business before or having debt for a property before) is not an irresponsible step for *me* (with my 20 years of building on these foundations).

Valuing each other's contribution. Some couples agree that one of them will stay home permanently and the other one will have a career. Some couples take turns working and staying home. Some people work in a business together. Some couples are both working in different careers, then there's a battle about whose career is more important. Whatever your situation, I'd say the person who makes the most money isn't automatically the most important. It's about how much value they contribute overall. Sometimes flexibility is more valuable to the family than finances. So have conversations around your contribution and the value you each bring to the partnership, then agree to respect each other's value.

Making assumptions. This applies to all areas of your marriage, not just finances. So often we assume that things will be done a certain way, probably the way our parents did them growing up, or something that we've seen work for other people. Your partner has their own set of assumptions and they're probably different from yours. So you both need to acknowledge that you've made assumptions and be willing to question them. Where did that assumption come from? Who said we have to do it that way? Besides, if you love somebody, I just think it's nice to ask.

INVESTING IN YOURSELF

I read *Rich Dad, Poor Dad* before I was 20, and got interested in property. I bought a block of units before my parents had bought their house. People often ask my opinion on the best thing to invest in. Although I don't give advice or share opinions, my answer, based on my experience, is always the same: invest in yourself. I've had better returns on myself than I've ever had on property.

What do I mean by investing in myself? It's not just putting money into your own development and your own projects. I value my time more than money. I invest in myself by putting my time, energy, and focus into improving myself and making a success of the things I commit to. I think I'm the most valuable asset that I have.

So I have to get very disciplined about what I say yes to and what I say no to, and there needs to be a lot more no than yes. I know my nature and I know that when I say yes to something, I'm going to stick to it. No matter what, I'm going to be obsessive about it and make it work. So I set myself up for success by choosing things that I think are good bets: timing, values, passion, and purpose.

Choosing well and doing whatever it takes to succeed at that—in other words, betting on myself and then investing in whatever growth I need to do to make it work—I think that's the best way to move my family forward. I get to be happy doing what I love, which makes me a better wife and mother. And when I invest time and energy into making my businesses work, I know I can make enough money to provide the lifestyle I've promised my family.

I get to choose how to do that. I believe in business, so right now I'm spending my time creating great businesses. I choose what I want to focus on in that space, and I don't ask for permission. I've earned the right to do that, from years of being the provider. So I pick what I want to do and I do not apologize.

When it comes to financial assets, I do believe in diversifying and having a mixture. I like diversifying my income, too. I've committed to earning a certain amount to uphold our lifestyle, but it's up to me where I get it from.

I believe in giving yourself room to breathe, especially if you have a family. Not only do you have a responsibility to give them a bit of security, but it's not fair on your partner and kids if you're on edge about finances all the time and you bring that stress home. But I also believe in a small element of fear, because fear does drive me.

I have a problem with the way some people invest in businesses, throwing big checks at them without even making them show that they have a viable product. Maybe this is why I love sweat equity over investing capital for early-stage startups. A lot of money is very nice, thank you, but it won't necessarily create a business that's efficient and geared up for profit and growth. A business without fear is like a rich kid who never had to work for anything, as opposed to the kid who had to work two jobs, get a secondhand car, and understand what it's like to drive a shitbox until you get somewhere. Having that big check is like going into a BMW dealership and saying, "I'll have one off the floor, thanks." I don't like scarcity mentality, but I love what a little bit of fear can do.

So give yourself breathing space, but don't be afraid to take calculated risks and back yourself. If you don't, who will? You don't need to ask for permission, as long as you're covering what you promised to your family. The rest is in your control.

MY PERSONAL RULES AROUND FINANCES

I don't like to make rules for other people, but I do have some personal rules that guide the way I do finances. The number-one rule is to cover my commitments to my family. After that, it's just a question of deciding which numbers matter to you and what you need to do to hit the targets you've set for yourself. Are you prepared to do that? Once you've covered everything in those first two categories—commitments to your family, and targets you set yourself—the rest is yours to play with.

FIRST, COVER YOUR PROMISES

Your number-one responsibility as a breadwinner is to provide for your family. You'll have a whole lot of commitments around that, whether it's keeping the house or paying for certain schools or anything else that you've promised your family they can expect. There's a minimum amount you need to cover expenses, and it's your job to come up with that.

The breadwinner has the ultimate responsibility for the family, but they should also get the ultimate freedom. As long as you're keeping all your promises, it's up to you how you do it.

I've promised my family that, for the foreseeable future, we'll continue to live in the home we've got and travel and do all the other things we're used to doing. But I never promised them that I'd stay in the job I'm doing right now. Sometimes I don't know what I'm doing next; I know better than to make any promises about that. I just say, "I'll keep you posted. I'm not sure myself." I've made sure that if something happens to me, my family will be taken care of. So I've covered my responsibilities and I've given myself permission to explore.

Sometimes I take risks, but I know that I can always go back to the circle I was in before. Yeah, if I decided to just go back to working in my marketing agency, it might take me three months to build up my clients again as a marketer, but I could do it. To be honest I'd rather not have to do that, but if I found myself in a situation where I had no other choice and I had to do it to fulfill my promises, I would. Knowing what your fallback is can actually be a driving force to succeed. I've got a backup plan but it's not something I want to do, so I'm motivated to keep moving forward.

You've always got options. If I decided tomorrow to quit my job and not do anything else for 12 months, I could put my units on the market and sell them and live off that money, for example. As long as we kept the house and the kids were fed, that'd be my prerogative.

TRACK YOUR MAGIC NUMBERS

Call in the Coach: Emily on Financial Simplicity

Based on your own values you need to determine what's meaningful for you. If you're not clear about what your numbers actually are, get some clarity. Then cut out anything that's overcomplicated.

Tamara loves that she is the source of her own financial ability. She gets to choose how much she earns and from which sources. Not everybody thrives on that diversity; some people care more about consistency and simplicity. Your personal finance model needs to be a reflection of your values and what's important to you.

As I said before, everybody has a different opinion on what numbers matter. This applies in your business and with your personal finances. You don't need to track every little financial movement down to the cents and get obsessed with every possible metric. You just need to know what your "magic numbers" are and keep an eye on those.

You and your partner might decide some magic numbers together. For example, you'd know what your magic number is for covering your mortgage, another number for living expenses, and a few other numbers you pick together, like how much you want to be able to put aside for overseas holidays, or to support another family member, or to put toward a shared goal like buying a vacation home. Whatever it is, you know that if you've hit those magic numbers, the rest is just detail. You can track it if you like, but you don't need to overthink it.

You might periodically check in and report on your magic numbers with your partner. Mortgage paid—check, money for expenses—check, vacation booked—check, savings—check. Or whatever it is that you've agreed. If you've done all that, you can go and play.

GO AND PLAY

When I'm talking about finances, I think in terms of BAMs—bare-ass minimums. How much do I need at a minimum to cover my expenses? Then once the BAMs are covered, am I delivering on other promises? Am I servicing family goals?

If you can answer yes to all those questions, the rest of your resources—time or money—are yours to do what you want with. You can choose to work more, earn more, and decide how to use that money. Or you can choose to invest your valuable time in something else that you want to do.

Cover your BAMs, keep your commitments, then go and play.

Coaching Exercise: Money

WITH EMILY

The first recommendation when it comes to managing your finances is to go back to the goal-setting chapter of this book. Financial success is an area of life that's really measurable, so it's relatively straightforward to set tangible goals and use your goal-setting strategy to achieve them.

If it doesn't feel as simple to you as naming your goals and adjusting your actions, you might benefit from doing some deeper work around your mindset as it relates to your finances.

Here are two suggestions for exercises that will help you with that:

FINANCIAL EXERCISE #1: BREAKING THROUGH BELIEFS

This an exercise to do *once*.

In this exercise you'll identify all of your negative self-talk and blocks around money.

Focusing on the negative isn't a popular approach in terms of positive psychology, but we don't give a shit about positive psychology when it comes down to the fact that the truth is

(Continued)

(Continued)

more important than anything else. If you're having a problem with money, you need to own it before you can solve it.

Here's how to do it:

Write down all the negative beliefs you hold around money. For example, statements like: "I never earn enough," "I'm a bad saver," "I'm too irresponsible to be financially secure," "I'm too chaotic to manage money well," "Emergencies always come up and drain my savings," "Other people are limiting my financial opportunities," "Money is evil," "Only people who are born rich have money," "There's nothing the world would want to pay me for."

For each belief you've acknowledged, write down all the evidence you have that this is true. When has this happened to you? What were the circumstances? What behaviors do you do over and over again that show this statement is true?

Then, for each belief, think of an example of a person you know of who's proved that belief wrong. If you wrote "only people who are born rich have money," think of somebody who was born into poverty and became rich. If you wrote "I have to work 80-plus hours a week just to make enough money," think of somebody you know who has a comfortable lifestyle and only works 40 hours.

Now imagine that you're that person. Imagine what beliefs they would have had to give up to achieve what they've achieved. Of course you won't know what they actually think, but put yourself in their shoes and use your imagination—that will "bridge" your worlds.

The aim of this exercise is to give you an awareness of the ideas you're carrying around and how they're limiting you. Unless you are really stubborn or actually traumatized, this awareness should trigger your subconscious to start formulating new behaviors around money.

If you've done this exercise and you find that you still need some help unraveling your beliefs, try exercise #2.

FINANCIAL EXERCISE #2: MONEY MINDSET RECONDITIONING

Pick a statement about money that embodies the opposite of one of the beliefs you wrote in the first exercise. Don't limit yourself to writing a realistic goal—this statement doesn't have to be measurable or achievable. It can be something that seems completely improbable. You can basically write down your fantasy, with no strategy and no probability of the universe delivering it to you in reality. For example: "I am an extraordinary saver." "I am amazing at managing my money." "I earn $500,000 per year."

Put the statement in the present tense and put yourself in it. "I, Emily Diamond, am an amazing saver."

Write it out 15 times a day for at least six months.

Observe the results of your experiment.

I strongly recommend this one if you're having trouble breaking through a mindset about money. Examples where this might be helpful would be: if there's a limit to what you feel you deserve, if you think your earnings are restricted at a certain level, if you have habitually negative behaviors around saving and spending, or if you think you're not a certain type of person with money (e.g., "I'm not the type of person who could have an investment portfolio").

If any of that sounds like you, try the daily written reconditioning.

If you've tried both of these exercises, and you still feel stuck or gross around money, there are deeper unconscious issues. I recommend getting a coach to help you.

Building your bucket list: Finances

Here's where you start a list of things you'd like to do or have, related to your financial capacity. They don't just have to be

(Continued)

(Continued)

about seeing certain numbers in your bank account. There might be an asset you'd like to own, an experience you'd like to afford, or a way you'd like to be generous to other people.

Examples to get you started:

Pay off all my student debt.

Buy a vacation home at the beach.

Teach my kids to manage their money.

Generate multiple income streams.

Sponsor a child's education.

Travel overseas twice a year.

Pay off my parents' mortgage so they can retire.

Grow an investment portfolio.

MY BUCKET LIST: THINGS TO DO FOR MY FINANCIAL HAPPINESS

1. _____
2. _____
3. _____
4. _____
5. _____
6. _____
7. _____
8. _____
9. _____
10. _____

CHAPTER **13**

"Thanks for asking"

How to name expectations, make agreements, and carry your own bags

I got married the first time when I was 22. It was very quick; within a year of meeting each other we were engaged. He was 15 years older than I was and he turned out to be a bit of a narcissist.

The more successful I got, the more difficult the relationship got. He would put me down and I started believing him. It wasn't good for my head. But you choose these things; I definitely chose him.

But then I chose out. I decided I wanted to be happy and I wasn't going to compromise any more. We broke up after nine years of marriage and everybody thought I was crazy. But I think the partner you're with should think you're the best thing in the world.

Florian was so different. He was raised by a working mother and he's got two sisters, so he's open-minded about gender roles. He thought it was great that I didn't want to be a stay-at-home mom. He really wanted to have babies. You just know when you know. Florian's perfect.

I'm talking about marriage in this chapter because I'm married and a lot of people are. But I just mean a significant relationship where you share a life and home and you're committed to one another. Whether it's heterosexual or same-sex, whether you have kids or not. and whether you've had an actual wedding ceremony or not, you know the kind of relationship I mean.

You might be reading this chapter as a single person. You might not plan to get married, or want to get married, or you might just think it's never going to happen for you.

Or you might have been married already, and think "been there, done that." I did.

Sooner or later most of us, for some significant period of our lives, are going to find ourselves partnered up with another person. And if you're a self-supporting, rising woman who knows her values and knows her value, your life is probably pretty full. Arranging it around somebody else is a huge ask. It's not easy, and it's worth thinking about what you're prepared to put into it and what you want to get out of it, before you dive in.

If you've already got a partner, there's always room for change; it's inevitable in a lifelong relationship. If there are areas in your relationship that aren't working—aren't aligned with your values, aren't serving your personal pie—there are ways to shift them. You're only ever one decision away from changing your life, or one conversation away from changing your relationship.

When I met Florian, I said I didn't want to get married. I'd been married before, and to me the premise of marriage and what society classed as a wife was something I didn't want to buy into again. I assigned a certain meaning to marriage, and it was a life that I didn't want to live. I ended up getting married again after I realized that I could actually just do it my way. Marriage is different for everybody and this chapter is about the way that my marriage works—and it does work.

I've noticed in some marriages that people seem to feel like they can't evolve, like "this is how we were when we got married, so this is how it stays." But people keep changing constantly, so your marriage should, too. Through your twenties, thirties, forties, fifties, and beyond, what's important to you and what you enjoy keep shifting. The marriage needs to keep up if it's going to survive.

So I don't think you should get married based on things that will change. Don't choose him because he's got a good job and he provides a great life for you to have together, because that could all change in a second. It's not in your control. My marriage with Florian is based on our values. We both agree that that's why we want to be married: we want to be married to each other's values, and to who we are as people, but we have no idea where we're going to end up.

When we first got married, he was a 100% stay-at-home dad (I chose to have kids with him before we got married because I thought that was a bigger commitment), and he thought entrepreneurship was the scariest thing in the world. He'd look at me and say, "I'm so proud of you, and I'm never going to do that!" He was so adamant. Now, 10 years later, he's got the bug and there are days I think he's more interested in business than I am. Nothing's shifted for us as far as how our marriage works, because our values are still the same. But he's been invited to experience something through witnessing it in me. His perception on entrepreneurship has changed because I've shared my experience with him—which is really cool, right?

It's not as if we're now both high-flying businesspeople and our family life will take a backseat. Neither of us is concerned about where this might take us, because we both encourage each other to do what we want to do, and we know our values mean that we'll prioritize the life we have together.

SUCCESSFUL WOMEN INTIMIDATE MEN

That's what we've been taught to believe, right?

For a long time I downplayed my success. I think we sometimes put on an act in order to not intimidate people or make them question their own lives. Isn't that all we're doing? People go straight to comparison, and you want to protect them—and yourself—from that. At some point I started trying to own the fact that this is my life and this is how I choose to do things. I decided I wasn't going to apologize for my success, and more than that, I was going to own it.

Ironically, the day I started owning it was around the time that things started to fall into place for me. It felt like it lifted a fog and started attracting the right sort of people and opportunities into my life. I suddenly had an influx of people who came into my life and became my tribe. I don't think that's a coincidence; I think you attract what you put out. And all of a sudden I wasn't an alien any more. I didn't have to worry about intimidating the people around me, because they were all owning it too.

If you're in a heterosexual relationship where the woman is more "successful" than the man, it can feel really uncomfortable, because we've been told that there's a certain standard for each gender: men work, women look after children. Men earn more money than women. We accept that as the truth, and start to conform to it from a very young age. If you're going to do things differently, you need to recondition yourself. It's almost like a detox of the thinking you've been raised with. Start questioning it: Is this my view? Is this what I chose, or has this view been chosen for me? Is there somebody else out there having a different experience that resonates with me more than the "normal" I've been shown?

The beautiful thing about Florian is that he's never once been jealous or intimidated by my success. He's just riddled with happiness and pride. He also knows that what he's doing, raising the kids, is so important. He thinks of it as a job. When we go to business functions where I'm not known, everybody talks to him first, automatically assuming that he's the business owner and I'm the spouse. He's completely confident in delivering that line: "I'm a stay-at-home dad." He owns it. They usually don't realize it until some tie-in, which is fun to watch unfold.

When we worry about our careers "intimidating" our partners, we're actually not giving men very much credit. To some degree they have the power to create their own options and choices; they could probably choose to earn more or pursue more ambitious career goals if they really wanted to. There are two people in the relationship, both of you making the decisions together about how you're going to run things. If he's 100% confident in what you chose, you should be, too. And remember, above everything else, he chose you.

SETTING EXPECTATIONS

My relationship is based on a whole lot of spoken and unspoken expectations. (All relationships are.) Some of them are things we've decided together, and some are things that one of us has just assumed, without verbalizing it.

If you've set an expectation together, you should keep that promise to each other for as long as it works. And if it stops working for you, you can't just stop doing it, but that's when you can go back to your partner and renegotiate. Otherwise they're still operating under the original expectation, and if you don't let them know you want to change it that's when you get conflict and breakdowns.

If you never talked about the expectation, you can't assume it's set in stone. Sometimes you both want the same thing and you don't need to talk about it, which is great. But if one of you is not happy, they're allowed to put their hand up and say, "Hey, I never agreed to that!"

We used to have this arrangement where my parents came and stayed with us every second weekend until Florian said, "Why do they have to come every second weekend?" I responded with, "That's the weekend Dad's home from the mines," and he said "Yes, but when did I agree to give up every second weekend to spend with your parents?" I realized I'd never asked him to agree to do that; I just assumed he would.

Our strategy is to renegotiate our expectations every 12 months. We sit down and each write a big list of all the things we feel obliged to do, that we're not happy about. I think of it as a spring cleaning for our mutual obligations. People talk about the seven-year itch; I reckon it's more like a seven-year list! If you let it all go unspoken, you end up getting stuck with things you didn't agree to and you resent your partner. After seven years the list can be long and ugly.

So once a year we write it all down, the big things and the little things, then we go through each other's lists and we renegotiate. We acknowledge that we've got a finite amount of time and energy and resources to share with each other, but we can always negotiate a deal that works for both of us.

For example, a few years back I said to Florian, "You're not keeping the house clean. I like it clean when I get home, I can't stand getting home and picking up after two kids after a day at work. That's really important to me." He said, "Okay, but you have to understand that it's really hard to do that with two toddlers. I could do it with one, but two makes it a lot harder to keep that commitment. So I need you to give me an hour's warning before you get home. It won't work if you show up without warning and expect the house to be clean. And you need to be a bit more relaxed while we've got toddlers, until they can start picking up after themselves." That was the deal we made: he would do his best to have the house clean when I got home, if I gave him an hour's warning that I was coming. And if I didn't give him any warning I wasn't allowed to be upset!

Writing down a list of all your grievances and then presenting them to each other sounds like a recipe for the biggest fight of your marriage, doesn't it? Here are some rules to keep the conversation on track:

- When you're bringing up a problem with your partner's expectations, first take responsibility for letting that behavior form, and accepting it.

Two people created these circumstances, not one. The other person might have inflicted it on you, but you probably sat back and didn't say anything—otherwise you wouldn't have gotten to this point.
- When it's your turn to present an issue, calmly state the problem, how it impacts you, and what you'd like to renegotiate it. Keep it simple and don't let it spiral: when you bring up a problem, suggest a solution, too. This isn't a forum for complaining.
- Neither of you is allowed to argue with the other person's feelings. If somebody says there's a problem, it's a problem. It's your job to work together to fix it.

Once you've negotiated and made new agreements, you can hold each other to them through the year.

During one of those sessions we made a rule that we wouldn't commit to any regular activities on weekends. We decided that if we were going to free up those weekends by not seeing my parents, then we shouldn't fill them up with other shit. So the kids have to do all their activities between Monday and Thursday, and we both agreed to that. If Florian booked the kids for something on a Saturday, instead of starting a fight I'd just say, "Hang on, that's not our agreement. You'll have to call and cancel."

Having preexisting agreements we can point to makes it so much simpler to resolve things when they come up, because we've already decided—together—where we stand. Alternatively, you can have a discussion about a change to the arrangement *before it happens* and decide together on whether to break it on this occasion.

This is the absolute core of what keeps our marriage together: knowing how to have conversations, negotiate with the resources we have, and set expectations. And once we've decided something, we have to stick to it or come back and renegotiate.

Coaching Exercise: Making Agreements

WITH EMILY

Agreements are just a simple set of expectations and conditions that you articulate together, which can be reviewed if things are not working.

Agreements don't just apply to romantic relationships. In case you haven't realized, your life is one giant set of agreements. Agreements make societies work. Countries have agreements with other countries; citizens have agreements with their governments. The legal system is a set of agreements.

Wherever there's a workable system, it's built on agreements—and personal relationships deserve the same opportunity. So you might find it helpful to set agreements in other major relationships in your life, like with family members, close friends, and colleagues.

Here's a step-by-step guide to setting healthy agreements:

STEP 1. BE AWARE OF YOUR AGREEMENTS

We fall into a lot of social agreements unconsciously. For example, in a lot of relationships it's automatically assumed that the woman is the main caregiver of the children or the manager of the household. These are social "agreements" that we didn't necessarily agree to; they just exist.

As well as the agreements you've taken on board automatically, you'll have agreements you've verbalized and chosen to participate in.

To identify your existing agreements in a relationship, list all the things you're currently doing for the other person that would cause an upset if you didn't do them. If your doing or not doing something would cause a problem with your partner, you know it's an agreement. Everything you come up with in that category forms your list of existing agreements.

STEP 2. IDENTIFY FLAWED AGREEMENTS

Look at the list and circle all of the agreements that do not work for you. These are things you hate doing or resist doing. Things that don't honor your values. Anything that makes you feel disempowered, resentful, or upset in any way should be circled.

(Continued)

(Continued)

For example, my husband and I kept coming up against the same problem in our relationship: I would tell his family things he didn't want them to know about, and he would do the same with my family. Through having the same conflict over and over, we realized that we had an agreement in place that didn't work. We'd each assumed the agreement: "You belong to my family now, so I can treat your family like mine and vice versa." But the way we were interacting with each other's families was causing conflict.

We reworked this and came up with a new agreement: we can debate how to deal with something with respect to our families, but at the end of the day he gets to make the final call on his family and I get to make the final call on mine. I'm the bridge to my family, and he's the bridge to his family. We identified the assumed, flawed agreement and replaced it with a defined agreement that makes conflict much less likely.

STEP 3. DRAFT NEW AGREEMENTS

Once you've identified what doesn't work for you, think about what would. What would you be willing to offer in that area of the relationship? Be specific about what you'd be willing to agree to do with your time, energy, money and other resources you have to share.

Also draft a list of needs you'd like the other person to meet. What would you like to ask them for that you think they would get some pleasure or satisfaction from doing for you?

For example: I hate laundry so much. My husband hates cooking. So he does all the laundry and I do all the cooking, and we agree that the other gets to choose how they do it. I can cook all the meals in a week or order in, and he can launder whenever or take the laundry to the Laundromat. We don't judge.

STEP 4. SET AGREEMENTS TOGETHER

Once you've prepared, call a meeting with the other person and make new agreements together.

Don't just ambush them with the concept of agreements and your list of requests. Give them the opportunity to prepare their own list to bring to the table. Otherwise, it's likely they'll either refuse to participate, or default to your list of agreements without having the headspace to communicate their own needs properly.

There are no rules restricting what you can make your agreements about. With your partner you might have agreements about domestic arrangements, parenting, sex, communication, your families of origin, or anything else that's significant to you both.

STEP 5. REVIEW

Agreements are similar to goals in that when you make them, you can't predict what's ahead. As your relationship evolves or life changes, your original agreements might not work any more, so agreements can and should be reviewed periodically.

It's a great idea to review your agreements once a year. Through the rest of the year, you can modify them as needed. A fight is often a trigger to make a modification to an agreement! Fighting (which can also be expressed as silent treatment) is a sign that we've dishonored each other's values or broken an agreement. An argument or breakdown in any relationship is an opportunity to review your agreements.

CONDITIONAL AGREEMENTS AND UNCONDITIONAL LOVE

The danger with making agreements is that it can become a point-scoring game. "I kept all my agreements but you didn't keep yours." "You didn't come to my awards night so I'm not going to your sister's birthday." "You didn't do the laundry so I'm not cooking dinner tonight."

The thing is, two healthy individuals should each be capable of meeting their own needs without help. You don't need to do things for each other, but you've chosen to enter into a relationship where you offer to do those things. When one of you lets down their side of the bargain, the other one should still be able to operate independently, without heaping guilt on the other person.

This is why we like to talk about relationships being 100/100, not 50/50. Thinking of it as 50/50 places conditions on love. It demands that the other person puts in their half all the time and that everything is scored, fair and equal. It's saying that I'll do something nice for you if you do something nice for me.

But if both people bring 100% of themselves to the relationship, they can love each other unconditionally. You're each 100% responsible for yourselves and the way you interact in the relationship; you're not dependent on how the other person interacts. So you can choose to keep your agreements, or not, regardless of how the other person upholds theirs.

Some agreements operate on conditions, like "I'll have the house clean if you call ahead." That's fine if the conditional agreements are made from a place of unconditional love. If your partner breaks the conditions of the agreement you might withdraw your side of it, but you won't withdraw your love.

Upholding your side of the agreement is just as much about respect for yourself as it is about the other person. Your promise to keep your agreements, and keep loving unconditionally, is a promise that you make to yourself. Fulfilling it is a way of expressing yourself as a 100% whole, rising individual.

CARRYING YOUR OWN BAGGAGE

Loving unconditionally is not the same as meeting all of your partner's needs, all of the time, whether they're doing anything for you or not. Making healthy, conditional agreements gives you the freedom to say "no, thank you" to things you aren't prepared to take on.

For example: We have a rental property. We were thinking of selling it, but Florian wanted to keep it and said that he'd take care of all the property maintenance. So I agreed that would work. Now that he's started working on his own business, that maintenance stuff is annoying him because it's taking him away from his key focus. He doesn't want to be around there cleaning the pool and talking to tenants. That's understandable.

So I said to him, "Okay, you don't want to do the maintenance any more, that's fine. What are the options? Do you want to sell the units or can you afford to outsource the maintenance?" He came back to me and said that he couldn't really afford to outsource it because his business hasn't taken off yet, but he's hoping it'll be making good money in about a year's time.

So I offered to call the bank and change our payments on the property to principal-only for 12 months, and we could use the difference to pay for the maintenance. It's not coming out of my earnings, because the maintenance is his responsibility. But that's something I can do for him to give him an extra 12 months to find a way to afford it. In a year he'll start paying for it, go back to doing it himself, or we'll sell the units. I'm not willing to pay for it myself because that means I'd have to work more hours. I could easily push myself and keep piling on more shit I need to pay for, but our agreement was that if Florian wanted us to keep the units he would take care of the maintenance. So we come up with a way to meet that obligation without impacting me, because I wasn't the one who changed the agreement.

As soon as you feel like you're carrying somebody else's bags, that's when things go sour in the relationship. So just define what your luggage is. What are you willing to carry? If you want to pack 20 fucking suitcases to go to Bali, you'll end up lugging them up a sandy hill and not having fun. Don't turn to him in that moment and say, "Oh honey, could you help me with my 20 bags?" Not if he decided to pack light. You chose your own bags. You packed them. So unpack some shit, make a decision to get rid of some stuff, or hire a porter. But don't expect your partner to carry your bags.

PROBLEM SOLVING

When times are tough, that's the best time to build culture. That's true in business and in marriage.

They say it's a lonely job being the CEO. I think that's an old-school saying, said by stale CEOs. In my businesses, I'm pretty transparent with my team. They know what we're making, when we're winning, when we're losing. That means that when something goes wrong I don't have to yell. Most of the time they're disappointed that they've let me down, because they've got the full picture of what's going on and what it means.

If you didn't have this transparency, it would be lonely to be the CEO. That's how businesses used to be run (some still are). Employees never knew if things were going badly. The executives would maintain this image of being in control and being untouchable. Then people would turn up to work and the doors would be closed and they'd be out of a job, and they'd go "we didn't see that coming!" My team would see it coming. We'd have so many conversations about how to fix it, and whether we wanted to keep going.

It's the same in marriage. You don't want to come home one day and find that the locks have been changed and you didn't see it coming. You want to be super clear so there are no surprises. But you need to create a safe environment for talking about problems, the same way you do in the office. My employees know that I don't mind if one of them brings me a problem. They know that I'm a problem solver and that's what I do. If a staff member comes to me and says "I've made a mistake and I don't know how to fix it," I'm not going to yell at them. Of course I have to hold them accountable, but then I need to help them figure out how we get out of it together.

There are going to be times in your marriage where there's more bad than good. Your partner needs to feel like they can tell you things that are probably going to hurt you. At work these conversations aren't as emotional, but at home it's really hard. It's very difficult to be disciplined, think logically, and work through it as opposed to just losing your shit. But I'd rather my husband came to me and told me, for example, that he wasn't finding me attractive any more, than if I came home six months later and found the locks were changed. That's why it can be helpful to have personal rules and policies, just like you'd have in a work environment.

For example: In my marriage we have the "jealousy rule." We're both attractive people, we both spend a lot of time hanging around the opposite sex, and we know that we're constantly going to find ourselves in situations that present an opportunity to be unfaithful. We're both in different countries, on planes, on different time zones all the time. We know that if either of us were to have an affair it'd be easy to do it without the other one finding out, but we also know that we don't ever want to be without each other. And we've agreed that infidelity would be a deal-breaker.

So having acknowledged that we both have the opportunity, and knowing that it'd be a dealbreaker, our rule is that we just don't make jealousy part of our relationship. We don't keep an eye on each other or get concerned about that, because it's exhausting. If one of us is worried, we say to the other one: "I've noticed this. Should I be worried?" And we can reassure each other, but that's as far as the conversation goes. There's no checking up or obsessing or jealousy.

I don't hold anything sacred when it comes to other people's marriages; you have your own rules. If you know each other's values, you know the things you need to share with your partner. You know what shit's going to worry them and upset them. You know when you're doing something wrong because you get that feeling in your gut. That's just a warning sign to say that something's not right.

If you're committed to the relationship, you need to have a proper conversation and it needs to be mediated. I'm a huge believer in facilitators and coaches and mediators when it comes to having hard conversations in business. Your marriage can benefit from the same things.

Building Your Bucket List: Romance and Marriage

If you're single, heartbroken, or not interested in love, you can still own your happiness in this area. What does it look like for you to be romantically and sexually fulfilled? Where do you find human connection? What makes you feel sexy? How can you be the love of your own life?

If you're partnered, the same kinds of questions apply. Think about what you want out of a relationship and how you're going to create that for you and your partner. What type of marriage do you want to look back on at the end of your life, and what are you doing to create it?

Examples to get you started:

Go on a date once every two weeks.

Get counseling so I can be a better partner.

(Continued)

(Continued)

Go to Paris for our 25th wedding anniversary.

Surprise him every year on his birthday.

Create a tradition as a couple.

Model a loving marriage to my kids.

Learn to be emotionally independent.

Renovate a home for our family together.

MY BUCKET LIST: THINGS TO DO FOR MY LOVE LIFE

1. _____
2. _____
3. _____
4. _____
5. _____
6. _____
7. _____
8. _____
9. _____
10. _____

CHAPTER 14

"Mommy, don't go!"

How to get over guilt and be the parent you want to be

A few weeks ago Florian went to Hong Kong for a week. Our older daughter struggled with him leaving because—as she said to me—"next *you'll* leave us." (I had a trip to America booked for when he got back.)

I reminded her that Papi is usually home all the time so we should let him have his trip.

"But *you're* not," she said, "so I don't want *you* to go."

Talk about mommy guilt. This is one of those moments where you can either crumble under the weight of it or rise above it.

So I told her again about the reason I was going to the States. I'd been asked to show one of my products on QVC. I talked to her about how this was one of my goals that I'd been working toward and how excited I was to go.

She saw how excited I was and how important it was to me and she said, "Well, can I come?" I thought about it and realized it wasn't so complicated, since my sister lives over there. I called my sister to check and she said sure, she could take my daughter to school with her to help with her first-grade class.

So while Florian was on his flight to Hong Kong I booked a flight for me and our daughter to go to the United States. When Florian landed he saw the booking and texted me: *What a great idea to take her! So happy for you. It will be a lovely experience.*

Having separate overseas trips with our kids once a year was on our bucket list. Seems like I kicked this goal!

GUILT, MYTHS, AND EXPECTATIONS

As mothers, we're always self-guilting. Just the other day I was getting on a plane and my little one was screaming, "Mommy, don't leave me!" (Of course, 10 minutes later my husband sent me a video of the kids laughing their heads off.)

A whole lot of our stress around parenthood comes from making assumptions and worrying that we're not enough. We believe cultural myths about motherhood and feel the pressure to measure up to certain expectations—whose expectations? Half the time it's shit we've made up in our head. We tell ourselves all kinds of stories, like:

I can't be a good mother if I don't spend all day with my children.

My kids will have abandonment issues if I travel without them.

If I want to have kids and keep working, I'll have to compromise.

It's not fair to my family if I pursue my own goals.

I have to stay at home because I'm the mom.

My husband doesn't want to help with the kids.

And we make up assumptions about what we think the other moms on the playground think of us. Or how much we imagine our kids are suffering when we're at work. Or something our mother-in-law said.

Don't let anybody else tell you what a mother "should" look like, especially other mothers. They get uncomfortable if our version of mothering looks different, because it challenges what they believe about their own lives.

My favorite is when I'm out somewhere without the girls and another woman says to me, "Where are your children?" It's not a genuine question. It's not like they're saying, "You know, I really admire you and I aspire to be a businesswoman and a mother like you. Can I ask you who helps look after the kids? How do you make it work?"

No, that question—"Where are your children?"—assumes that I don't care. Like I need to be reminded; like I'm going to say, "Oh my God! Where *are* my children? I must have left them at home! They came out of my vagina but I forgot all about them."

It assumes that *they* know what caring looks like, and I'm not doing it properly. As if being a mother is like being a Girl Scout and I haven't got all the right badges. They're going, "Here's my 'I baked the cookies' badge ... do you have that one? No? What about the 'I clean the toilet twice a week badge'? The 'I had to stay up until 2 a.m. making cupcakes for the birthday party' badge? Where's yours?"

Since I don't do chores, I'm going to have a pretty hard time getting any of those. Sorry to disappoint you.

Instead of trying to earn all those badges of honor myself, I throw away the assumption that I'm meant to be the source of everything my kids need. They've got a father, relatives, friends, teachers, and other parents around them. I want my kids to be a bit like me, but there's so much that I love in so many other people. Florian is so good at so many things. He's amazing. He learned his life skills from his dad. I want my kids to have a bit of that. And my kids can speak German—that's a sacrifice for me, because I don't understand them, but they got that from their father and I want them to have it.

There are different things, good and bad, that I want my kids to be exposed to. It's not all me. That attitude is so egotistical. It's like saying to your staff, "Right, you're only going to get training from one person for the rest of your life, and that's me." That's not how we train our teams. We tell them to go and get other mentors, listen to TED talks, read this book or do that program. Why wouldn't we want the same for our kids? Which is more important, doing *everything* for them to assuage our own guilt? Or letting their lives be enriched by all different people?

Making peace with your parenting choices comes back to knowing your value and knowing your values. If you're confident about what you can (and can't) contribute in different areas of your life, you'll know where you should be putting your energy and what you should delegate to coworkers, the nanny, or your partner. If you know what you need to do to stay sane and happy, you won't feel so guilty doing it. And if you live according to *your* values and *your* family's needs, you'll know how to answer people who criticize your choices, or at least you won't care so much what they think.

So don't be a slave to expectations. Don't assume you can predict what motherhood will be like for you or how it will change your priorities. And if you have a partner, absolutely don't assume anything about each of your roles until you've had the conversation! A lot of men would love to be invited to have more involvement with their kids, but they don't know how to bring up the idea.

Getting Over Mother-Guilt

My friend Sel on fueling herself, not her guilt:

I know what fuels me, and developing myself through travel fuels me. I travel a lot, without my family. People find that really hard to understand: How can I travel away from my kids so regularly? I find it strange when people say, "Oh, how did you get a free pass to go overseas?" I have a real issue with that, because I believe that sort of mentality is making your family like a jail, where you need to be let out. If I ever saw my family as something that restricted what I do, I would be resentful of that.

I've got three young boys, and I've always said to them, I'm nobody to tell them how they should live their life but I'm everybody to show them.

If I could only give them one or two pieces of advice, one would be to never settle. If you're not happy, don't just go "oh well, you know, I've married that person or I've taken this job or I live here now." Don't settle, because life is too long and too short. Too long to not make a change, and too short to not make a change.

Another thing I've always said to them is that if you have a dream, if you're passionate about something, you have to be all in. You have to give it everything you've got.

I tell my kids I've got no right to give them that advice if I'm too scared to take it myself. I'm very much of the view that if I looked at my kids and saw them in marriages where they couldn't do what they want to do, when the person who supposedly loves them is restricting them from being their best self, restricting their freedom, their individuality—that would break my heart and I would be furious.

I refuse to live that way. So my family knows that, and I understand that if I want to be the best mom for them then I need to do certain things for myself. I feel no guilt around that. I actually think guilt and kids are an awesome excuse to cover up your fear—fear of failure, fear of what people will think.

This "mother guilt" concept, I just don't feed that at all. I really believe that mother guilt does not serve you or your children. It serves nobody. It's not actual guilt because you haven't done anything wrong! You know that you haven't done anything wrong!

Of course I have moments where I'm like "I wish I was at the school presentation right now," but in the scheme of things it's more important to me to have a presence at something that actually matters. I don't overparent and overworry about that stuff because I think it doesn't actually serve anyone.

—Sue-Ellen (Sel) Watts

Founder wattsnextpx, wattsnext,
Your Secret Sauce, and zzoota
Vlogger of The Unconventional Life:
https://www.youtube.com/channel/
UCFhMSaKj43f0EXM-4b_H1DA

WHY YOU NEED TO STOP SAYING THE WORD "COMPROMISE"

The idea of "compromise" is a big one when people are talking about parenting. For working mothers, their whole lifestyle is supposedly one giant compromise. Going back to work means a compromise for your children. Or if you decide to stay home full-time with your babies, eventually your ambition whispers to you that you're compromising on what you're capable to achieve.

There are a few inherent problems with the language of compromise. First, it automatically assumes that you have to choose between family and business. It makes it sound like you either have to love your business more or your family more. And if a woman is playing a big game in business, she obviously must love her business more than her children.

That's pretty insulting. Of course all mothers love their children. Just because I run multiple businesses doesn't mean I love my work more than I love my kids.

The second problem is that assuming that we'll compromise forces a choice on us that we don't necessarily have to make. It might actually be possible to choose both: to love your business *and* your kids. You don't have to make the same choices as other people.

The reality is, you have *no idea* what's going to work for you until you have children. When Mia Freedman (who was the editor of Australian *Cosmopolitan* at the time) found out she was pregnant, she told her boss she'd hardly want any maternity leave. She couldn't imagine not wanting to stay in the loop and come back to work a few weeks after giving birth. But when her son arrived, work suddenly didn't seem to matter. She ended up staying at home for four full months, and it was a year before she came back to work full time.[1]

On the other hand, some women can't wait to be full-time mothers, but after a few weeks at home with the baby they're ready to throw that idea out the window and go back to work.

Emily on Going Back to Work

When I had my daughter I sent all my clients this letter that said I didn't know what was going to happen. I just did what Tamara would call blending—working out my values and integrating them. I still had a bunch of staff working for me, which was awesome, and I just had about six weeks of no meetings.

Then when my daughter was six weeks old we were running a seminar. Other facilitators I had trained were running those seminars, so I was just sitting at the back of the room supporting the facilitator and being there for overflow questions. That was the first thing I did back at work: go out at night to one of these seminars. Then I started going back to work in four-hour blocks that were really structured around breastfeeding.

The first time I tried to go back to work was for a whole day. I had this idea that one day a week would be really good, and my parents lived nearby, so they could help. The first day I was phoning my mom, just flipping out. It was the end of the day and even though I'd pumped, my boobs were all engorged and I was trying to get home and there was an accident and I was stuck and I was phoning my mom saying "I can't get back!" All these primal things were happening. I was panicking about not being with the baby, even though intellectually I knew it was fine. I wasn't fine. And my mom said this magic thing. She said, "instead of a full day, why not try two half days?"

And then I just gradually built it up to more and more. The girl I babysat when I was a teenager became our nanny.

Of course having children changes you. When I say you might not have to compromise, I'm not saying you won't have to give anything up for your children; that's not living in reality. What I'm saying is that if you organize your priorities in accordance with your values, you won't be compromising anything. If your values tell you that being home with your babies 24/7 is the most important thing in the world right now, taking a step back from work isn't really a compromise. If you know that you're making great contributions at work and you've got a trusted support network at home, delegating some of the mom duties shouldn't break your heart.

You might be surprised by your own capacity to handle both. Believe it or not, having a family has actually improved me as a business operator. It's made me a lot more ruthless with my time—if I'm leaving the building at 2 p.m. because I want to pick up my girls from school, I don't have time to waste at work. I make sure I get to critical conversations quickly. Having children motivates me to be a more efficient leader because I don't want to compromise time with my family or attention to my business. I want to do both.

Mothers are highly valuable to businesses because they tend to be highly organized. I quite often hear business owners say that they've hired a mother part-time and found her so efficient that she's almost offering the value of a full-time employee. Being a mother, you have to be that way.

So don't let anybody tell you that having a family and having a business will mean that you have to compromise. You won't know how family is going to change you until it does. But when it does, you might find that you can adapt without choosing one over the other.

I'm not saying that all women have to play a big game in business and raise a family without breaking their stride. Every woman's life is different, and some women don't want to do both at the same time. That's fine.

If you do feel you want to have a break from business to be with your family, be really honest about why that is. Put your hand on your heart and say, "I just want to take some time, selfishly, to exist in the family space and not the work space. I don't want to grow my business right now. I want to be a homebody." Or, "I've worked really hard my whole life, and now I want to take some time to just be with my family." Or whatever the reason is that's true for you.

But don't use your family as an excuse for not going after your career goals. Be honest about your choices. At different points in your life you might choose to focus on your business over family, or choose to put work on hold to spend time with your babies. That's great—it's your choice. Nobody is forcing you to do anything. Find a new way to talk about your choices, without using words like "have to" or "compromise." Make decisions that are right for you and your family, then own them.

You can't control what the moms on the playground think of you. But you can talk about expectations with the people who really matter—your co-parent and your kids. If you're feeling guilty because of a bunch of made-up expectations and lies you're telling yourself, you have the power to change the way you think and talk about work and motherhood.

We can check in with our partners about what their expectations actually are, and make commitments to each other that work for *our* family. We can reframe the way our kids see work and teach them to value it as part of who mom is. We can challenge our own expectations of what we have to achieve as a mother and what it means to love our kids.

REDEFINING SUCCESS AS A MOTHER

Unless you devote your every waking and sleeping moment exclusively to the care of your child and only have one child and literally

> *do nothing but spend time with that one child and focus your entire being on anticipating and then meeting that child's every whim, you cannot win at mothering. And if you did, imagine what an arsehole your kid would be.*[2]
>
> —Mia Freedman, Creative Director of
> MamaMia Women's Network

Women executives who responded to a *Harvard Business Review* survey on work-life balance[3] reported that the most difficult aspect of managing work and family was managing cultural expectations about mothering. Not necessarily *their own* expectations. But the cultural pressure they felt to "mother" in a certain way.

Modern parents—especially mothers—spend almost double the contact time with children that baby boomers did. But we also typically feel more guilty for not doing enough or not being present enough.

The only way to know if you're doing "enough" is to decide what enough is, *for you and your family.* Not for anybody else's family. Not compared to some undefined benchmark that you think you should be reaching. That's a great way to torture yourself, by not really knowing what the standard is, so you can never know whether you're actually winning or not.

I'm not downplaying the importance of spending time with your kids. I'm just saying that you don't have to bow to everybody else's idea of how it's supposed to look. You'll come up with your own ground rules for making sure that you're giving quality, consistent attention to your children. For example, Elizabeth Cronise McLaughlin (former Wall Street lawyer and now a corporate coach to high-level female executives) has a personal rule that she never misses bedtime two nights in a row.[4] I don't have that rule because I travel a lot. For me, I blend work travel with family time.

If I travel for two weeks or more for work, the family usually comes with me. When I do go away by myself, I extend my time away from the office for half a day per every day that I'm away, and spend some time with the family at the beach or somewhere away from home once I return. I go back to work with my batteries recharged. My executive assistant knows that that is nonnegotiable: if I'm traveling for business, she automatically schedules in a number of days afterwards for me to spend with the family before I come back to work. I think of it as working *on* my family, not *in* it, the same as I do with my business. I come back to work with my batteries recharged.

I get that not every mother understands this. Some women couldn't handle it if they couldn't see their kids every single day. Sometimes at school pick-up times, the other moms come up to me and pat me on the arm. "Oh, you poor thing, you had to go away again. Don't you miss them?" Well, I didn't *have* to go away, I *chose* to go away. The reality is that when I *am* with them I don't cook or clean and I spend every minute with them, taking them to the beach or doing other fun things. I'd rather have several days of uninterrupted quality time, with no chores, than be doing the school run every single day. But that's me.

Coaching Exercise: Create a Family Framework

WITH EMILY

The best way to succeed as a parent is to define your own framework and honor it. You get to pick the standards yourself.
For example:

How much contact time do you want to have with your kids on a daily basis?

What are you never allowed to say to your children?

What are your priorities as a family? What are your values? (Ours are silliness, kindness, and failure.)

What do you want to model to your children? What do you never want to model?

What do you want to give them?

What do you want them to learn?

What do you want them to experience earning?

What can they always count on you for?

This list of promises becomes the big circle inside which you parent. That's your focus. You don't need to feel guilty about any balls you drop outside of that circle. You don't need to feel like you're not doing enough, if what you're doing is enough to meet the commitments you chose as being the most important ones for you and your children.

Also: when you know what you've committed to providing for your kids, it's okay to delegate some of it to other people. We praise delegation in business; we recognize that effective entrepreneurs and executives have to learn to not do everything themselves. At work, not trusting anything to other people is an ego problem. Parenting isn't actually different.

So I have commitments around my child's experience of life, but I don't have to personally provide every moment of that experience. Instead I ask myself, how can I contribute to creating a loving and nurturing environment for her—with my time or other people's time? As parents, we can get falsely wrapped up in our own importance. Our whole life is interconnected with and held up by other humans. We can produce a positive experience of life for our child in a community, with the help of other people.

REDEFINING WORK IN THE EYES OF YOUR KIDS

We've all experienced the heartbreak of our kids saying *"Mommy, don't go to work."*

If my girls say that to me, this is what I say:

"You know how you go to school, and jiu jitsu, and see your friends and all those fun things? Well, this is my fun. Let mommy have her fun."

Don't be afraid to let your kids see you as a whole person. If work is a huge part of who you are, it's good to teach your kids to appreciate that about you. And you don't have to frame it as though work is in direct competition with family time. Of course if you come home stressed out, with no energy left for your family, your kids are going to resent your work. Instead, let them see that Mommy goes off to work because she wants to and comes home happy and satisfied, excited to see them.

It's all about framing work to your kids as an empowering thing, not a drag. Help your kids see that work is a good thing that contributes to the health of your family. Teach it to them as fun for grownups. In the same way you can teach them that their own hard work can be fun, starting with chores and homework and working up to entrepreneurial projects of their own.

I show them life design firsthand. Recently when I quit as CEO at one of my companies, the girls were devastated. I had to say, "No, it's a fantastic thing! Mommy's reinventing. Mommy didn't like being the boss." We had a big conversation and they got really excited, because they understood what I was doing.

I love saying to them, "I'm not sure what my future businesses will be but I know it will be really exciting. I have a list of the things that I enjoy doing like travel, wellness, and working with women in business, plus there are a few things on my bucket list I'm working on, like a book. I'm not sure what will come of it but I know it will be a great journey with a lot to learn."

Empowering Your Kids Around Work

Gina Mollicone-Long on teaching girls to follow their purpose:

I travel a lot. One day when my husband was driving all of us to the ski hill, my daughter blurted out, "I hate it when you go." The car got silent. I thought for a minute and then I said, "I hate it when I go, too. But one day, you're going to discover why you are here and what your purpose is. And I want you to pursue that purpose no matter who you disappoint or upset in the process, even if that person is me. I might not always agree with you but I will always support you. The world needs whatever you have to give."

I truly believed that it was time to start giving girls permission to follow their greatness. I wanted it to be easier for her than it was for me. On a related note, a few years later, we solved the "going away" problem by taking the whole family around the world for an

*entire year while I did a world speaking tour. It was
an amazing journey to 39 countries where my family
got to share in my work and be present at all of my
speeches. To use your brilliant word, I was "blending"!!*

—Gina Mollicone-Long, bestselling author
and creator of Greatness U

Coaching Exercise: Who do you want to be?

WITH EMILY

Parenting is a leadership scenario. I want to have more leadership influence over my child than an insecure friend, or a drug dealer, or an abusive boyfriend. I want my daughter to gravitate more toward me as an influence than to anyone else. For that to happen, I need to relate to her like I'm a leader.

Leadership is about consistency. If a leader is consistent you'll trust them and feel safe, even if you don't like them. So what kind of leader do you want to be for your children?

If you find creating a framework too dry, try this exercise.

Imagine how you want your kids to describe you when you're gone. Imagine if somebody asked, "Who was your mother to you?" What are they going to say?

Create that answer in specific detail. Who was I to them?

Then make a decision to move toward becoming the person in your answer. Remember from our goals chapter that a "toward" motivation is more powerful than an "away-from" motivation. Most of us want to move away from being like our parents, but that's not the most effective way to become the parents we want to be!

You can't guarantee that you'll always be the parent you want to be, but you can make a commitment to keep moving toward it.

REDEFINING GENDER ROLES

I think this is where same-sex couples have an absolute advantage: It isn't assumed who's going to do what; they have to sit down and have that conversation. The gender difference isn't there, so they actually have to have the conversation as individuals about what each person wants to do—do they want to work, stay at home, a mix?

—Sue-Ellen (Sel) Watts
Founder, wattsnextpx, wattsnext,
Your Secret Sauce, and zzoota
Vlogger of *The Unconventional Life*,
https://www.youtube.com/channel/
UCFhMSaKj43f0EXM-4b_H1DA

When I talk about having a stay-at-home husband, the reaction I've had from a lot of men is that they would love the opportunity to do it. The thing is, they've never been asked. Why aren't we having that conversation? We just assume we'll take on the roles that we've been taught. Instead we could each be playing to our core strengths and assigning our roles according to who happens to be better at what, or what we each prefer to spend our time doing.

If you have a conversation and get to choose your roles—instead of just getting landed with them—you're less likely to resent them. If you're a woman who earns more money than your male partner, that's a beautiful conversation starter. "Hey, there's been a shift in who the breadwinner is, so we need to have a conversation around the shift that needs to happen in our lives as a result of that."

If you've got a more demanding career than he does and you're contributing more money, you're going to have less capacity to give in other areas. The mistake most women make is assuming that we can keep up all of our traditional contributions at home as well as giving a lot to our career and providing for the family.

When I get home from work my kids are really excited to see Mommy, which is great, but Florian can't just put his feet up then because he's had a big day. That's not how it works, because I've had a big day, too. I don't have to pick up 100% from there on in. We both decided where we wanted to be during the day and gave that 100% of our attention. Now that we're back together it becomes 50/50.

Sure, sometimes I get home and he goes, "Babe, I've had the shittiest day and the kids are driving me insane. I need to go and read a book and be alone." And I say cool, I'll cover 100% tonight. You have a night off. It's not tit for tat, but he'll be happy to do the same for me in return the next time I come home and say "I've had a shitty day, I want to go and lie in the bath." Or like the other night when I came home and said, "I've had such a win today, I just want to celebrate, I'm not interested in doing school lunches or anything tonight!" He was cool with that. When you value each other, and you only ask each other to cover when it's really important to you, it all comes out in the wash. We don't keep a tally, but I reckon if we did it'd be pretty even.

Some roles you can't get out of, like being the one who has to be pregnant (if you're a woman), but you can choose to accept and celebrate those things instead of complaining. You most likely wanted to get pregnant—you didn't have to—and you were blessed to be able to do it. You chose to have children together and you knew what that would mean for you.

So don't make him feel guilty about it forever, and don't make your kids feel guilty about it. Just because you went through a lot of pain for them doesn't mean they owe you anything. The same applies to your relationship. Just because I work a lot and I'm the breadwinner doesn't mean that my husband owes me anything, or that the rules don't apply to me. He works hard all day at home. Outside of the nine-to-five, everything else we have to get done is a shared responsibility and is up for negotiation.

Men often struggle with the idea of giving up work, because of that drive to "provide" (even if they're providing in a different way, by doing all the hands-on work with the kids!). If you've never thought about the possibility of doing your roles differently, a dramatic shift might seem overwhelming. But remember, you've always got options and you're only one decision away from changing your life.

If the male in the partnership is driven to keep contributing financially, even while he's at home more with the kids, get creative! How can you maximize your resources to come up with a solution that works for your family?

If you have assets and need to leverage them to reward yourself this time off, then do it! Or downscale for a period. Or renegotiate your hours at work—you should have established your value by now, enough to demand some flexibility.

My friend Aaron on redesigning his life

My wife and I had three children in two and a half years. This year our son will turn five and our twin girls will be two. It's been an incredible journey and one that I've actively embraced.

You see, I stopped. I stopped working full-time and spent four and a half days of the week with my wife and kids. I redesigned how I worked. I was fortunate to exit one of my successful businesses and had worked hard to build an investment portfolio over many years that provides for my family.

The power of compounding investment growth and income along with a variety of company interests allowed me to stay home more and develop an awesome connection with my kids at the start of their lives.

It's time I can never replace. Worth more than any material possession I've ever owned. Do it again? You bet. In fact, my competitive advantage is I still have Wednesdays with my family.

—Aaron Zamykal, investor and entrepreneur

You might not have the same resources as Aaron, but I hope you're inspired to get creative about how each partner can contribute. Think outside the box, and do what's realistic for your family.

A good place to start the conversation is by talking about your personal pie. How much of your day is consumed by work? What are the things that fill your soul, that you need to do to be fulfilled? (For me, the main one is quality time with my kids.) Those two things need to be met and then everything else needs to find a way to sort itself out. That's how I negotiate with Florian: this is how much time I'm spending at work, this is how much time I need with you and the kids, therefore this is how much time we have left. Here's a list of things we'd like to do as responsible parents, property owners, and people. Right—what's on the table, what's off the table, what's nonnegotiable, and what can we live without?

Florian sees this time at home with the kids as a period in his life that won't last forever. In a few years our roles could change, and he knows that, so he doesn't feel like he's missing out just because he's not working right now. When it gets too much with the kids, he never takes it out on me. If I'm home late a few times in a row he might go "actually, I'd love to take a turn going out to dinner" and take himself out. But he never gives me the guilt treatment.

THE PROBLEM WITH PUSH DIAMONDS

Speaking of guilt: what is with a "push diamond"?

Giving a "push present" (often in the form of diamond jewelry!) is a growing trend, whereby the father is expected to give the mother a gift in return for her going through pregnancy and the birth of their baby.

Firstly, it's a new-age marketing fraud (like Valentine's Day). Secondly, it's designed to make us believe that our partners owe us something.

Yes, I get that the last weeks and labor are hard work, I get that some people vomit from day one, and I also get (firsthand) thinking that you're going to die in those last few minutes. But does that make our men owe us something? Didn't we both agree to this kid thing? Haven't we been dreaming of it since we were playing with Cabbage Patch dolls?

This concept of them owing us for something that is a downright privilege of being female, is absurd to me. Much like the men in the school playground who say "I would love to have spent time being a stay-at-home dad," I also think there are some men who (believe it or not) would love to experience making magic.

That's what it is—pure magic! We get to feel all the kicks, the movements, the birthing (which is, as they say, euphoric), and the bond that men don't get to experience that comes from giving birth.

So tell me again, why do we also deserve a diamond? I wouldn't trade giving birth, growing a child, and feeding them for anything, even if I could give up the tough moments in exchange. It's like anything worth doing: Does the good outweigh the bad? In this case it's the most magical (though sleep-depriving) time of your life.

The reward for me wasn't a diamond, and I would never expect one. My diamond was when the father of my child looked at me with such respect, admiration, and sheer love at what we had created—what I just delivered. There's something amazing about seeing a man turn into a dad in that second, and at the same time both having the same feeling of knowing that nothing will ever be the same again.

A shiny rock ain't got nothing on that.

But I guess it's what women think they deserve. That's a question of how you embrace the experience (good and bad). Would you really trade places with him if you could? Do you really want to be paid for your part?

I say we got the better deal ... so I think they're owed a consolation prize!

Building your bucket list: Parenting

I want to acknowledge that this is an area of heartache for some women. You might want children and not be able to have them, for a variety of reasons. Or you might be struggling with the decision to have children or not.

Or you might just not want to have kids, which is a perfectly valid way of being a woman.

If parenting isn't for you, feel free to skip this one. Alternatively, you might want to create opportunities in your life to exercise your maternal instinct in a way that isn't traditional parenting. There's a lot of power in being an auntie, a mentor, or a benefactor, and you probably have a lot more time and energy to give to it than those of us who have little kids of our own.

Examples to get you started:

Take my children to five different countries before they grow up.

Find an adult we trust to leave with our kids for the whole weekend, then do that once a year.

Write my own definition of parenting success.

Help each of my kids start a small investment portfolio on their 21st birthday.

Teach my children about my cultural heritage.

Sponsor a child overseas and visit them.

Take my children to work and teach them about what I do.

Help my kids to write their own bucket lists

MY BUCKET LIST: THINGS TO DO FOR MY CHILDREN

1. _____
2. _____
3. _____
4. _____
5. _____
6. _____
7. _____
8. _____
9. _____
10. _____

Florian's Story

I was working in front-of-house management in a hotel in London when Tamara walked through the door to check in. I don't know what it was, but it was like "whoa." I pushed my receptionist out of the way so I could handle Tamara's check-in. I didn't know what it was but there was something there, and during the check-in I could see that she must have felt the same.

When she left the next day she was about to get into the taxi, but quickly came back to the desk and gave me a five-pound note and said, "here, that's for you." And off she ran, seemingly embarrassed, and jumped into the taxi. I opened it up and there was a note inside with her email address, "In case you want to catch up when I'm back in London."

We emailed back and forth a couple of times and then she called me out of the blue. Soon enough we talked daily, then twice a day, three times, four times a day. We just chatted and

(Continued)

(Continued)

chatted and chatted. After a few weeks we were talking about when we would see each other again. Then one morning I woke up and checked my emails and there was a plane ticket that she sent me.

So we met in Australia. Her success didn't scare me away at all. If anything, it suited me in a way. I've never been really that career-driven. I'm starting to become that way now, but back then I certainly wasn't. When I was a child I remember saying, "I could be with a wife who works, and I can stay at home with the kids." I'm not sure where it came from, but I had those thoughts very early in life. "I would love that, staying at home with the kids and not having to work"—that was obviously a kid's perspective, but I was always open to that. So I guess I was sort of predestined for that role.

Six months after we met, I moved to Australia and got a job as front office manager. About 10 months in, Tamara called me at work. I'll never forget, I was in the service elevator between the 15th and 16th floors and she told me she was pregnant. I got out at the 16th floor and I was just there in the service area for half an hour, talking to her on the phone.

And then we had the conversation about whether we were going to get a nanny. I didn't think much about it at first. Let's just get a nanny, continue what we were doing, without even thinking it through, costs and all that. I'm pretty sure it was me who eventually brought up the idea that I could stay at home. I just threw it out there one day, like 'maybe we could try.'

We agreed that I would take a year off; I'd take paternity leave, just so I had a way out in case I didn't like being at home. That caused massive problems at my work. They weren't happy at all. HR caused me a few issues; it went back and forth because they were fighting it. It was unpaid leave, but I guess they just wanted to either keep me or fill the position with somebody else permanently.

(Continued)

I heard about it at work almost every day: "Florian, you're going to hate it." One of my managers said, "My daughter is six years old and I love spending time with her now because we can really talk, but all that baby stuff—it's so boring, you're going to hate it. You'll be so bored." How wrong he was ...

So I basically did the whole "mom" thing straight from the start. Tamara was really really busy. She was only working from another unit downstairs at home back then, but she still had to work most of the day, so she didn't come up much. I gave bottles at night, I slept in the baby room for the first few weeks, and we did this silly thing where we didn't want her to get used to a pacifier so instead of a pacifier we would give her our little finger ... I would stand there literally for hours during the night with my arm resting on this really uncomfortable bed rail to comfort her when she was crying.

We used to have very strict routines the first couple of years. We had this book; everything was organized in 15-minute slots. It worked so well, she was sleeping through the night from very early on. Then our second daughter came along and the book went out the door; it was too hard to build a baby routine around a then almost three-year-old toddler.

I met a few other stay-at-home dads over the years, but all of them started later in their child's life, doing a year of it here or there; no one I met did it right from birth and all the way through to school and beyond.

I think the feeling of missing out occasionally caught up with Tamara a bit later, after a year or two. I sent her photos and videos every day, so she was always in the loop, but I think other people were in her ear about it too.

A few years later the kids would do this theatrical cry when she left for work, "I don't want you to go." But literally the moment she left they were fine. It's the same at kindergarten. You drop them at their classroom and it's a big deal, but then you leave the room and listen from behind the door without them seeing you and they're fine within a minute or less. I've heard that from so many parents. It's the same now when I go away. They tell me

(Continued)

days beforehand that they don't want me to go and how much they're gonna miss me. I don't think anyone is taking any emotional damage from it, it's just part of life.

I often heard other moms complaining that they have the kids all day, Dad comes home from work, and they've still got the kids all night because the kids apparently don't really warm to their dad. They still want to spend time with Mom because they've formed that close bond. So it's like a full-time job and the dad often isn't involved too much.

For us, the moment they hear Tamara coming home, it's "Mommy's home! Yay!" And all three of us would shout that!

That's one thing I've always loved. Mom is always the mom. It doesn't matter how long she works and how much time they spend with me, that mommy role is just so ingrained in the kids. It gives me a break at night and it ensures that the kids have input from both me and her. They get both, which I think is great. They're very much used to both of us.

We do lots of vacations and weekends away. We've made an effort to go away for a week at least during school holidays. There was a time at the beginning where I let Tamara do a lot of things with the girls on the weekend without my involvement, just because I felt she had so much to catch up on. Now a lot of the time I just ask her, "Do you want me to come or do you want to have some time with them by yourself?" Most times we end up all being together.

Tamara organizes all the presents and the birthdays. I never touch birthdays. I cook most of the time. There was a stint where she cooked for a while. I always did the laundry right from when we were first together, because clearly I was much better at it, no disrespect. I've taken that over from my dad. He used to do a lot of the laundry at home, too, and I still remember him explaining to me how it all worked, which clothes go at what temperature, what goes into the dryer and what needs hanging up and so on.

(Continued)

I still get cranky when occasionally Tamara takes all the things and throws them together into the wash.

I think the girls got a lot out of having a dad at home. They got to do a lot more boy things. I do a lot that Tamara wouldn't or couldn't do, just typical dad stuff. I don't think it harmed them in any way at all, quite the opposite actually. For them it's just normal. So even recently when I started doing my own work they said, "What do you mean? You don't work. You're our dad, you're not meant to work!"

I've had lots of men saying they'd love to do what I do and I've had men looking down on me and then literally walking away from me when I explained what I do. Fair enough, there's probably not a whole lot in common, just different outlooks on life, I guess. I never took it personally. I have the same with women as well. I get some women saying, "I could never let my husband do that. I would never want to miss any moment of my child's life. I can't believe your wife is letting you do that." Like I'm taking something away from Tamara. And then I get the opposite, where women would say, "That's so cool you get to do that. I wish my husband would be more involved."

I get that a lot in the playground when I do the girls' hair. I've literally had women come up and go "Wow, I'm amazed to see a man doing that stuff. My husband wouldn't even know how to put a hair tie in." I've got a lot of memories of my dad taking care of us at home. He would always braid my sister's hair in the mornings. It was always my dad driving me to school and picking me up. I guess I had that role model from early on.

Sometimes I would turn up at a playgroup and all the moms would bitch about their husbands, about them leaving early for work, not helping enough, and so on. I can't stand that! I always thought, that's how it is, you decided to stay at home, that's your job. I'm sure the husbands are having a hard time at work, too. Everyone's doing their bit for the family.

Now that both my daughters are going to school I have started my own business. I'm really excited about it at the moment, going through phases where I'm either staying up until

(Continued)

one or two in the morning or going to bed earlier and then actually getting up before sunrise, which is between four and five here in Brisbane. I actually prefer that, having a few hours when everyone else is still sleeping and the house is so quiet. I can then fully concentrate on my work with a fresh mind that hasn't been loaded up yet with the usual day-to-day challenges or incoming emails. I've also noticed that I am a lot more relaxed on those mornings when the kids wake up grumpy. Fortunately, the rest of my family likes to sleep a little longer, so that works out well.

Years ago I never wanted to run a business. I thought, "I don't know anything about it and it's really not in my nature." But being around Tamara and so many entrepreneurs, going to all these business functions and trips around the world, lots of people would ask me for advice. I'm there thinking, how am I qualified? But I come up with ideas, they listen and implement, and that's cool. At the end of the day we're all just people who do crazy things, listening to and learning from each other, and I have learned to not put people on a pedestal just because they are more successful than me in one area of their life.

—Florian Loehr

NOTES

1. As told in M. Freedman, *Work Strife Balance* (Sydney: Pan MacMillan, 2017).
2. Ibid.
3. Harvard Business School, "Life & Leadership After HBS: Findings from Harvard Business School's Alumni Survey on the experiences of its alumni across career, family, and life paths" (2015), www.hbs.edu/women50/docs/L_and_L_Survey_2Findings_12final.pdf.
4. As told to A. Lancaster, "Making Room for Baby: Discovering You're Pregnant 3 Months After Launch," *Forbes*, February 6, 2013, https://www.forbes.com/sites/thebigenoughcompany/2013/02/06/making-room-for-baby-discovering-youre-pregnant-3-months-after-launch.

CHAPTER 15

The Business of Family

How to build culture and be a leader at home

Imagine if we talked to our colleagues the way we talk to our husbands:

Staff Member:	You look upset. What's the matter?
Me:	NOTHING!
Staff:	Okay ... well, I just came to tell you that I'm going on my lunch break now.
Me:	WHATEVER!

Imagine if you did that! They'd change jobs. So why do we think we can get away with talking like this at home?

If you're the breadwinner in your household, you're most likely a pretty amazing woman. You're probably in a position of some power at work. If that's true, you must be a good leader. You'd have to be good at managing people and resources, and being assertive without losing your shit, and empowering people around you to work toward common goals. If those things weren't true, you wouldn't be as successful as you are.

So why does a professionally empowered woman get home from work and stick her "I'm taking everything personally" hat back on? I do it, you do it, we all do it. We're not victims at work. So let's not fall into a victim mentality in our personal lives.

BUILDING CULTURE AT HOME

We spend a lot of time talking about the importance of workplace culture, and don't always give the same attention to household culture. What's the culture like in your home?

In business, we have all kinds of tools at our fingertips to keep our workplace interactions healthy: a company vision, shared values, policies about accountability, regular reviews, and communication techniques for having awkward conversations. I think it'd be a good thing if we brought some of these structures home.

Why not take the things we know about business culture to create a healthy culture in our marriage? Or adapt tools from the workplace, and make them work at home? We all invest in professional development for the good of our careers; let's give our relationships the same level of investment.

I'm not saying that you should be the boss at home or run your household like a business. I'm just saying that you can use some of those principles and practices to adjust your mindset and have a healthier home life. When you need to calm your emotional state and make a good decision, or when you need to have a hard conversation with your partner, that's when you can draw on some of the tools you've learned in the workplace. And it starts with building a healthy family culture.

Some families like to create a vision and mission statement together. You might like to put your family commitments up on the wall so you can point to them—just like you would in your company. Sometimes you have to be the visionary in your own house.

BE A PARTNER, NOT THE BOSS

If you're the boss at work—or even if you aren't—you're probably the boss at home, too. Women typically take on the role of manager in the household. Your husband might "help" a lot around the house, but you're the one who decides what you need "help" with. You remember when the bills are due, or nag him when the lawn needs mowing. He might do the laundry, but you probably remind him when you need something clean to wear on Monday. He might drive the kids to jiu jitsu, but you're most likely the one who puts things on the family calendar.

Excuse me, but who decided that you were in charge? When did that get negotiated? Is your husband your employee, or your partner?

We like to blame men for the unfair distribution of work at home. I'm wondering if they're as much to blame as we think they are. If a man lives with an empowered, capable woman who tells him what to do and how to do it, and loses it if he doesn't do things the way she would do it herself—can you blame him if he just lets her take over? If I lived with somebody who was better than me at doing household chores, and very specific about the way they wanted things done, I'd probably be quite happy to sit back and let them do most of the work.

The problem with appointing yourself household manager is that it sets your husband up to be treated like an employee, not like an equal partner in the marriage. Not only that, but in addition to managing all the household responsibilities, women typically do up to 80% of the chores themselves. I'm sorry, what kind of good manager does 80% of the day-to-day work? Haven't we heard of delegating?

Part of treating your marriage like a 50/50 partnership is giving over control of 50% of your shared responsibilities. You don't need to take over everything, even if you're honestly better at something than he is. We all love to tell our husbands how to do things. But will it kill you if he doesn't make the banana bread the same way you do? Isn't it good enough that he's doing it, so you don't have to?

Have you ever heard yourself saying, "Everything depends on me! If I want something done properly I have to do it myself! You have no idea how much I do around here!" These are the catchphrases of a nagging wife. We've all heard them or been guilty of saying some version of them at some point.

If you want a life where everything isn't dependent on you, you need to accept things done differently from how you would do them. Declare that to yourself: *I want a life where everything is not dependent on me.* Every time you feel like stepping in, remind yourself of that promise you made to yourself. *I don't want a life where everything depends on me, so I'm willing to accept it done his way.*

And if he really has no idea how much work you do around the house, show him. Let him take responsibility for his half of it so that he can appreciate what it takes for the two of you to manage your lives together. That means stepping back and letting him drop the ball sometimes. If you did all your kids' homework for them, would they learn anything? It sounds arrogant to talk about your husband that way, doesn't it? But the reality is that women often treat their husbands like kids who can't do their own homework, instead of treating them like grown adults. It's like it's in our DNA to take over everything around us.

Don't get me wrong: women are (generally) fantastic at household management. We tend to be really good at multitasking, and most of us are born organizers. Traditional gender roles are what they are, and they run deep. Women have always been in charge of running things at home, and typically we're incredibly good at it.

But just because you're the best at something doesn't mean that you have to be the one to do it. This applies at work and at home. Think of marriage as a team effort and yourself as a team player. The most qualified person on the team doesn't automatically get to do everything. At work we delegate responsibilities to the people around us as a way of empowering them, and freeing ourselves up to do more important things.

Sure, if you delegate something it often won't be done as well as you'd do it yourself. But I have a rule at work that if something's done to 70% of the standard that I'd do it myself, it's good enough. If somebody does something to 70% of your standard you're onto a winner, because you didn't have to do it yourself! If we applied the same rule at home we'd save ourselves a lot of trouble. And just because something isn't done your way doesn't automatically mean it's not good enough. Treating your partner like a partner means trusting the way he chooses to carry out his half of the responsibilities.

If you let go of tightly controlling everything, I guarantee you'll realize that your partner is actually better at some things than you are. Florian's definitely much better at a lot of household things than I am. But I'd never know that if I were trying to do it all myself.

EXPECTATIONS AT WORK AND HOME

Recently I was in one of my offices around the time that all my staff were going to lunch. The phone was ringing, but nobody picked it up because they were all trying to get out to have their break. Obviously I just wanted to go: "Oh my God, the phone is ringing and nobody's answering it. Hel-lo? Do you hear that?"

That's what I would have said at home. "The baby's crying, hel-lo? Am I the only one who can hear that? Where's your father?" I do it all the time.

But at work we don't say "The fucking phone is ringing, are you deaf?" Try that out and see how it works for you! How many staff do you think you'd have left? Instead we're disciplined about how we respond to things at work. We take a deep breath and make constructive comments, like:

> Hey everyone, I know it's your lunch break but the phone is ringing and that's a customer. Are we still committed to putting customers first?
>
> What structures do we need to put in place to make sure that everybody doesn't go to lunch at the same time? Because letting the phone ring is not aligned with what we're all committed to.
>
> It's okay, we'll let this one slide. Let's all have a chat about it after lunch so that we can avoid it happening again.

Imagine if you spoke to your husband more like that at home. Don't you think the conversation would go a lot better than, "Hel-lo, the baby is crying? Isn't it *your* turn?"

I didn't lose my temper at work because it wouldn't help the situation and it would damage my relationship with my staff. Isn't the same true at home? At work we have rules around communication and how it's acceptable to speak to one another. Do you hold yourself to the same standards when you're talking to your life partner?

I don't have a big blowup with my staff every time something goes wrong, because I understand they're only human. They get complacent, and so do I. In a healthy workplace you don't blame or dwell on that, you just figure out what you need to do to revitalize the culture.

As leaders at work, we know we need to keep reinforcing our mission if we want our people to stay committed to it. We don't explain the company vision and values at the job interview, then expect people to remember them three years later. We keep having those conversations all the time. We're constantly reviewing the commitments we've made together, as a team, so that we stay on track.

It can be exactly the same at home. You can't just tell your partner on the first day you move in together: "Okay, you'll be in charge of taking the trash barrels out" and then get shitty every time they're overflowing from that day forth. First of all, you need to check that he's okay with that agreement in the first place. Then you need to review it every so often and make sure that your expectation is still reasonable, and he's still onboard.

At work we call it a performance review. We sit down with our staff and say, "How's everything working out? Are you happy to keep going on the pathway we designed for you? What can we do better?" We check whether both parties are meeting their obligations, because we're a team. Nobody's yelling and throwing shit at each other, at least not in healthy workplaces. It's a positive conversation.

I'm not saying to treat your partner like he or she is an employee. I'm saying don't treat them *worse* than an employee. If you've got the skills to handle your own emotions and negotiate conflict productively at work, you can step up and do the same at home. Show your partner you love them by treating them with at least the same level of respect you would apply to an interaction with your staff or colleagues. If you chose to spend your life with them, they're probably worth a lot more of your energy than anyone you spend time with at work.

The basis of a healthy partnership is respectful listening. Emily has an exercise to help with that:

Coaching Exercise: Presence Listening

WITH EMILY

Every time somebody talks to you, your brain puts what they say through a ton of filters that match your model of the world. We all do this; we automatically distort, delete, and generalize what people say so that it's easier for us to absorb. What we hear is always different to what they say.

We miss A LOT and experience A LOT of drama because of our self-talk's nonsense.

Presence listening cuts down this filtering activity by overloading your brain with an alternative activity. Your internal

---

dialogue is automatically running all the time anyway, so you might as well give it something to do that will help you to genuinely listen.

Here's the alternative activity to keep your self-talk busy and stop it running amuck in your life:

Repeat every single word the person says as they say it.

This temporarily halts your distorted hearing. It forces you to really pay attention and it helps you to really hear what they say.

People resist this exercise because they worry if they're busy repeating what the other person is saying (in their mind) that they won't be able to think about it and form a considered response.

First of all, your brain is working on multiple levels all the time. Even if presence listening is dominating your internal dialogue, your brain is still formulating a response.

Second of all, most of the time when we're "listening" we're not actually paying attention in order to formulate a response. We're just being polite enough to wait for our turn! But not really polite enough to genuinely listen!

Those of us who are less polite will sometimes get too excited and just butt in—we all know people like this! (That's me raising my hand.)

If you start practicing presence listening, you'll be less in the drama of your internal dialogue, which is always spewing garbage at you.

You'll be able to respond to what's really happening, not what your brain tells you is happening.

You'll be deeply connected to people, and they'll feel respected—people can always tell when you're responding to what they really said versus what you think they said.

This exercise goes a step further than "active listening." Presence listening is really hearing.

Game on: We dare you to try this anywhere and everywhere, as much as you can in your life. If you really care about people, don't you really want to hear them?

HAPPY HOME, HEALTHY BUSINESS

The most important career decision you'll make is who your life partner is.[1]

—Sheryl Sandberg, COO of Facebook

I don't function well as an entrepreneur if I'm not feeling supported and loved at home. The two things are directly correlated for me. I'm sure this is true no matter what your relationship status is: if you're content and happy in your personal life, you're more likely to be confident at work. Your personal stuff shows up everywhere. So creating a stable, happy home life is part of setting yourself up for winning in business.

If I show up to work and I've had a fight with Florian, everybody knows! Coming to work grumpy from a fight at home is going to impact my day in the business, exactly the same way that it impacts my family if I get home from a shitty day at work. On the other hand, if I come home on a high from a huge win at work, we're celebrating as a family. And if I feel loved and supported at home, I'm unstoppable at work.

Your spouse might not be your business partner, but they are your partner in life. They can be your most important support as you navigate your career, even if they're not involved in your work at all.

I don't ask for Florian's permission when it comes to my business and my career, unless it impacts the family. He knows that I love family time and really guard it, so I'm not going to make decisions that eat into my quality time at home. He's reassured by that, and the workings of it don't really interest him.

What does concern him is when my friends know what's going on in my work life before he does. Things move fast in my world, and a lot of my friends are involved in my businesses, so sometimes they know what I'm up to first. If something major happens for me at work and he hears about it through somebody else, you can see his bottom lip drop.

Whenever he feels like that, he knows to call a "Baileys night." It's this tradition we've got, where he'll come home with a bottle of Baileys, and when I see it sitting there I know that we're going to stay up until 3 a.m. and drink the whole bottle together. Usually on a weeknight! We'll sit and talk for five hours, and it's not five hours of arguing and debating, it's me going, "I'm so excited, I've got so much to tell you!" And him saying "Yeah, me too!" And we'll share what we're thinking and bounce ideas off each other. That's what we do, whenever we feel like we're not connected.

We try to share everything. He doesn't want me making business decisions that affect the family. I don't want to miss out on parenthood. I'm still a mom, and I still very much want to know what's going on with the kids all the time. He doesn't make any critical decisions about the kids without asking, and in return I don't do that about business for him.

MIXING BUSINESS AND PLEASURE

I think it's a total myth that if we want to keep our professional image intact, we have to pretend not to have a personal life. (Remember Sallie Krawcheck and the pink nail polish?) "Don't mix business and pleasure"—that's bullshit! If you love your work, business is a pleasure. And if you have a spouse who you love too, you can invite them in to share that with you. I think when we let our personal life filter into our work, it enriches the way we do business.

My career presents a lot of opportunities to travel away from the family. Florian and I see these trips as things I'm committed to because I'm passionate, not things I'm obligated to do because of business. I always ask permission from him if it's going to impact him and the kids, but I tend to only accept offers that give me the opportunity to blend. Most people around me know not to bother inviting me unless it's a blending thing. They know I won't go too long without the kids, and that I like to take my husband with me on trips. We love to go on planes together; we call it a "date flight."

So I always invite Florian to come with me if I can. Sometimes he says he'd love to come and other times he's not interested, and then I decide whether I want to go without him or not. He's never once told me I can't go. I don't have to ask for permission, it's never "Can you look after the kids when I go away?" Instead the conversation goes: "I have a trip, of course you're invited, would you like to come?" If he says no, he knows he's staying at home with the kids. There's no begging and pleading and getting one up on each other. It's never like "you just had a boys' weekend, now it's my turn." That's toxic!

You're probably wondering how we manage to go on trips together when we have two kids. Sometimes we have family to look after them.

Sometimes we take them with us. Other times we go via New Zealand and drop them off with their grandparents, so they can have time together. We just look at the options each time.

It's been harder since the kids started school, but while they're in elementary school we figured that an experience in another country is pretty good exposure for them. We decided that we don't want to pay for private elementary schooling and instead use the money to invest in experiences that help them be worldly and streetsmart. We had a discussion about that and agreed to it.

I'm very conscious that our kids are growing up in a bubble. We are on an island. By the time they finish school, I want them to have a bigger perspective and be responsible enough to look after themselves. We're rearing adults, right? We're trying to empower them to be able to survive on their own. So we will pull them out of school unapologetically, because to us the experience of traveling to non-English-speaking countries to experience different cultures is just as valuable as school. And you can take homework anywhere.

My husband gets that my career is one of my great passions, and my kids are starting to understand that too. When exciting things happen in my work life, we all celebrate. And I see my work as part of a bigger plan for our family.

Something that's brought me and Florian together over the past few years has been that we both have bucket lists, and we love to see each other tick things off. Now our kids have started their own lists.

Blending my work life and my family life isn't just about taking the family on trips; it's about all of us having a shared vision, and working on it together.

Building your bucket list: Home

What kind of home life do you want to have? Which values do you want to teach your kids? What agreements do you want to have with your partner?

Think about how much time you want to spend at home and at work, what you need to be happy at home, and how you can be a team player with your partner and a leader in your family.

MY BUCKET LIST: THINGS TO DO FOR MY FAMILY CULTURE

Examples to get you started:

Write a family mission statement with my partner and kids.

Give up control of one area of our home life and let my partner lead it.

Create a family tradition around one of our shared values.

Write my partner a letter of appreciation for the things he/she is better at than me.

Do something fun together as a family every second weekend.

Write a list of family resolutions every New Year and help each other to achieve them.

Think of one thing I need to be happy at home and ask my family to provide it.

1. _____
2. _____
3. _____
4. _____
5. _____
6. _____
7. _____
8. _____
9. _____
10. _____

NOTE

1. S. Sandberg, *Lean In: Women, Work and the Will to Lead* (New York: Alfred A. Knopf, 2013).

CHAPTER **16**

Territory versus Tribe

How to foster friendships that bring out your best

When we talk about "community," we're often thinking about "territory."

We think that "community" means knowing your neighbors or being in the PTA at your kids' school. And if that's meaningful for you, that's great. But I don't think about my community in terms of how far away or close they are. I measure it in terms of the **value** people bring to my life.

Community means "being together as one." It's whatever makes you feel that.

A NEW WAY TO EXPERIENCE COMMUNITY

People talk about finding your tribe, which is just finding like-minded people who share your values. My tribe is entrepreneurs. My tribe is people who challenge me. If I'm not a little fish, I'm not happy. I'm driven by feeling out of my depth. So I'm probably not going to find my tribe in the street where I live. My people are all over the world.

It might seem like a difficult thing to stay connected, because of the distance, but I don't look at it that way. I think about travel time versus wasted time, the time you waste by choosing mediocre. I've set up my life so that my offices, my girls' school, and the airport are all within 10 minutes' drive of my home. I'm not commuting every day like some people are. I refuse to commute because I can't commit to spending two hours every day in transit. But I can bundle that time and choose to use it for travel time when it suits me. I can't commit to a daily commute, but I can commit to traveling once a month or so. It's just taking the same amount of time and energy that I would have spent anyway, and directing it more effectively.

It's similar to the way I grew my haircare brand, Hot Tresses. There are two approaches I could have taken. I could have gone down the typical route of selling it through hairdressers, and knocked on a whole lot of doors to get a whole lot of small distributors in Australia. It would have taken a huge amount of time and effort, and I probably would have grown it to a two-million-dollar business.

But I always do the opposite of what everybody else is doing. Instead of going the normal route, I looked at the niche and the marketplace—globally—and decided I'd do better by sleeping overnight on the plane to LA, having those same conversations with distributors like Nordstrom, and growing my business into a 30-million-dollar one. It's the same amount of effort. I just thought, "Do I want to sleep in my bed and wake up in Brisbane to knock on doors all day, or do I want to sleep on the plane and wake up in LA?"

LA is also my favorite place to blend. Some of my closest friends live there, so my trips include great times with amazing dining and nightlife, quality conversations about business with like-minded entrepreneurs, and exploring new opportunities for my brands. Some "me" time without the kids and hanging with girlfriends is also good for my soul.

It's the same with long-distance friendships. I'm seeking out the tribe that I want, and I don't care where I need to go to get it. It's the same amount of energy for a better result. I don't care if they speak a different language than I do, or come from a different culture, or live in a different time zone. I make it work. Friends don't need to be geographically close. Just because somebody lives in my territory doesn't mean they're a good person for me to be friends with. If there's no chemistry with your existing network, seek out something else. Forget about territory boundaries and think more about what kind of friendships match your values and meet your needs. Everything else is a detail.

FROM LIKES TO MEANING

In a world of digital "connection" focus less on connecting and more on "moments of connection."

—Paul Dunn, Chairman of Buy1Give1

In our world—Facebook, WhatsApp, LinkedIn—it's all about making connections. But does the connection ever turn into anything deeper?

I don't really do Facebook personally, only for business purposes. I value people's time, so I'm also mindful of the value of what I'm sharing. I think most people are just posting their highlights reel. I'm not a gloater. I do have moments where I look around at the amazing things I'm doing and think "Yeah! If I posted this on Facebook, I would *so* win." But the people who matter aren't finding out about my life from Facebook.

Having friends all over the world means doing a lot of digital communication. A really great side effect of our obsession with our phones is that you can feel just as connected to your long-distance friends as you do with the ones who live two streets away. You're less likely to notice the distance these days. Plus I'm a night owl, so communicating in the LA time zone works perfectly!

Some people say "I like to post on social media because that way all my friends can keep in touch." But do you really need to post it on social media when you could just post it in a private group, or share it on WhatsApp?

We call Facebook contacts our "friends." But are they really? I want to move away from "likes" and "friends" toward real friendships and real meaning. I like to share my wins with my closest friends—my tribe—but you don't need to shout it to the whole world.

Technology can do great things for building community. When geography is less important, your options become really beautiful. But I think we should be selective with what we share on social media, the same way we're selective with our real-life friends.

BLENDED FRIENDSHIPS

I hate it when people say to me, "I know you're busy, but ..."

Or when I'm passionately sharing about something I love in my life and they react by saying "Wow." Not the kind of "Wow" that means they're genuinely amazed and excited for me, but the "Wow" that says they think I'm a crazy dreamer. They say things like "Oh, you're intense," or "I don't know how you do it," or "How do you fit it all in?"

Or my favorite: "No wonder I haven't been able to get ahold of you!"

All of these phrases tell me that the person doesn't understand me at all.

When you say "I know you're busy," I hear emotional manipulation. I hear you telling me that you expect me to act as though I'm more important than you. It sets me up to feel guilty and respond out of that guilt. I just feel slimy.

And, "No wonder I haven't been able to get ahold of you"? Is there anything more needy than that picture, of somebody wanting to get a*hold* of you? If I wasn't available, it's because I had higher priorities at that moment. That's not a reflection on you, it's just everybody's reality—we all have different things going on that we have to manage. It doesn't mean I love you any less. Empowered women will always tell you where you stand, so you don't have to guess all the time. A friendship with me is a very transparent one.

When you ask me, "How do you fit it all in?" I hear that your perception of me is that I never stop, that you think I don't know how to look after myself. In reality I think I get more downtime, rest, and self-care than most people I know.

I do have moments of flurry where I go, "I'm jumping into that Ferrari! I want to fucking drive this car as fast as I can because I'm so excited about it!" I have moments of inspiration that provoke heaps of activity. But the next moment I'll become a breastfeeding hermit who just wants to sit at home and nurture my children, to the point where my daughter says, "Okay, Mommy, I think you've made up for all the kisses you missed out on."

It comes and goes in cycles, and I have no idea which part of the cycle I'm going to be in at any given time. If I didn't blend everything, I wouldn't have the flexibility to cope with it.

People who know me understand my values. They know that I really value quality time with friends, so they know I'm never too "busy" for that.

And they understand that I blend, so they try to pick a moment to blend our friendship into something else. They'll say, "How's your week looking? Can I tag along to something?" or "This is what I'm doing, where can we fit in together?" They know that I'm going to maximize my day, but they also know that I'm going to have moments of downtime. They check in on how my blended week is looking and where we might be able to overlap.

I tend to do my friendships during work and school hours so that I get to honor my family. If it's a weekend thing, I bring them all together.

FRIENDSHIP RED FLAGS

Just because some people are nice to you doesn't mean you should spend time with them. Just because they seek you out and are interested in you or your affairs doesn't mean you should associate with them. Be selective about whom you take on as friends, colleagues, and neighbors. All of these people can have an effect on your destiny.

The world is full of agreeable and talented folk. The key is to keep company with only people who uplift you, whose presence calls forth your best.[1]

—Epictetus, first-century stoic

I have a group of friends, but I don't have an abundance of friends. I'm not still friends with the people I went to high school with. My friendships are intentional and aligned with where I'm at in life right now; they don't just happen to me. I'm very selective about who I spend my time with. My friends impact my mental health, and I bring them into my home, which is a sacred space.

I not only let friends into my home; a friend is somebody I'd invite to my house without doing a lot of preparation. If somebody is coming over and I feel like I have to tidy up, or change my clothes, that's a red flag. That's a warning that I don't feel comfortable in this relationship.

Another warning is if I feel like I have to put on a special persona for somebody. I don't have different faces for different people. You can't compartmentalize each section of your life—business, different friends, family, whatever—it gets too exhausting, because you've got to remember the rules for each section. I have the same values across all my life, and the same rules for engagement across all my life.

I don't like being called to show my worth. If you don't value me, I don't have to show you that I'm valuable. If you listen to somebody else about my worth, I'll leave the relationship. I don't have to prove myself.

If somebody doesn't understand your worth and vice versa, then you're not aligned. Move on.

I don't like it when people ask me, "What do *you* think I should do?" Don't look at me. What sort of life do you want? That'll tell you what you should do. I don't like it when I hear my friends telling each other what to do. I don't find it healthy.

My rule is "experience-share only." If somebody said, "Do you think I should leave my husband?" I might say, "Well, my experience is that I stayed in my first marriage for too long." But I'm never going to tell you what to do. If you feel the need to do an opinion dump or if someone requests this because they are "stuck," be sure to declare it first: "This is my opinion, take it with a grain of salt, and here's where my opinion is coming from."

Conflict happens in a healthy friendship. To have a great relationship you need to share some core values and challenge some of each other's values. Otherwise there's no growth, and you don't get a kick out of being together. If you have too many conflicting values your friendship won't work. But even the best of friendships will have some healthy tension. If I'm growing, and my friends are growing, we're going to trigger stuff in each other. When that happens, it's a cue for me to ask myself—is there something in myself that I need to look at? Or have they got something going on that I need to support them through?

Women can erode other women's power base so quickly. What a horrible responsibility. In empowered friendships, we assume the best of each other. If there's a conflict, we have faith in each other that we're trying to do the best thing by each other. Everything else is resolvable.

Coaching Exercise: Go on an Acquaintance Diet

WITH EMILY

The word *diet* has a lot of baggage for women, obviously. A lot of us don't find it healthy to use that word when we're talking about how we relate to food, but "dieting" doesn't have to be just for food. We can find new power in the concept of a "diet" when we apply it to other shit in our life that's keeping us captive.

How about a diet from looking in the mirror? Or a body-shame diet? How about a makeup diet, or a social media diet?

A couple of years ago I went on an "acquaintance diet" for a year. I didn't contact or spend time with anybody I considered only an acquaintance; instead, I devoted all my time and energy to meaningful interactions with valued friends.

You can "diet" from two types of acquaintances, online and real-life:

Online Acquaintance Diet.

Go through your Facebook friends and unfriend anybody you haven't had an online interaction with in a year.

As you go to unfriend them, notice how it feels for each person.

Are you hesitant to delete them because you fear judgment?

Or do you feel like, "Oh my God, I'm going to miss this person in my life"? If you feel that way, you need to reconnect with them.

Real-Life Acquaintance Diet

Make the decision not to spend time or energy on anybody you haven't seen for two years.

You might want to go through the contacts in your phone or address book and physically delete them.

Again, as you go through the list, notice how you feel about each person. Who does it feel good to let go of? Who do you fear letting go of, and why? Who do you need to reconnect with, instead of deleting them?

Setting Intentions

Once you've let go of all those old contacts, you'll have a sense of new space in your life.

Whenever we create space, new stuff inevitably comes in to occupy that space. If we're not intentional about what we put into that space, any old bull that's floating around is going to fill it up.

It's the same with friendships. Now that you've created space for your relationships, set intentions about who you're going to bring in to fill that space.

(Continued)

(Continued)

What's your intention for your friendships? What role do you want friends to play in your life? (Remember, if you're blending, friendships can meet multiple needs in your life.) How can you spend time with friends that challenge you and nourish you? What kinds of interactions have the most meaning?

Going on an acquaintance diet isn't just about cutting people out; it's about letting people in. It's a framework for who you let in, and who you let go.

Building Your Bucket List: Friends and Community

Is this an area of life you do well, or are you longing for more connection? Do the people you spend time with honor your values and help you to be who you want to be? How can you create memorable experiences for the people you care about? What work do you need to do on yourself to be a better member of your community?

Examples to get you started:

Take my best friends away on a holiday we've always talked about.

End a relationship that has run its course.

Join a professional organization that stretches me.

Quit social media.

Surprise each of my close friends with a special experience on their birthday.

Join a group of people who share the same interest I do.

Have dinner with my old friends once a year.

Write a manifesto for my friendships.

MY BUCKET LIST: THINGS TO DO FOR MY FRIENDSHIPS

1. _____
2. _____
3. _____
4. _____
5. _____
6. _____
7. _____
8. _____
9. _____
10. _____

NOTE

1. Epictetus, *A Manual for Living*, a new interpretation by Sharon Lebell (New York: HarperOne, 1994).

CHAPTER 17

Why Blending Matters

How to get laser focus to create your legacy

Everyone goes through the same stages when they have a business.

First, you're excited and scared.

Driven by fear, you manage to survive.

Then you start to thrive. And during that stage you probably go through a phase of paying yourself back for all the hard work you've put in. You buy yourself toys and houses and all kinds of shit.

Eventually you start asking yourself, "What does it all mean?" "What's next?"

Four out of five businesses fail. I've survived. 1% of businesses make a profit of over $10 million. I've joined those ranks. I've gone from survival, to thriving, and now to focusing on my legacy.

I believe in two things to my core:

1. Business will drive positive impact in the world, and
2. I need to encourage women who are playing a bigger game for profit, by helping them follow their purpose without compromise.

As a mining girl from a small country town in Moranbah, how can I help? I lead the way. I lead by example. As an investor, I only partner with founders and acquirers who believe in the Buy1Give1 Model of business (more on that later in this chapter). I step out of my comfort zone and share my experiences. I connect with other entrepreneurs so we can empower each other to think big. I surround myself with an amazing support team, so that I have lots of cuddles and cushions for when I'm up against the haters, the controllers, and the no-change-makers.

Most importantly, I get really good at saying no to things and people that don't contribute to either of the two things above. It's amazing how much power and energy comes from defining your purpose and the legacy you want to leave. It gives you laser focus and a reason to jump out of bed in the morning.

That's why the blend is so important. It's not just about having an easier life, more freedom to do things you want, more earning power, more respect, more time with people who matter, more fun, more playtime, more indulgence ... those things are some of the bonuses of a blended life, but they're not the endgame.

When you know what you value and you know what value you bring ...

When you know what your purpose is and what you want to leave behind for others ...

... your focus becomes crystal clear.

Blending helps you live a life that's in alignment with that focus. It helps you serve the most important things, and cut out everything else.

My legacy is a work in progress. So I've invited people I respect to contribute to this chapter, including my mentor Jeff Hoffman.

Jeff is a serial entrepreneur who has received numerous awards for his lifetime contributions to the field of entrepreneurship. He's also produced Hollywood movies, concert tours for high-profile artists, and a Grammy award–winning album. He serves on the boards of multiple charities and nonprofits, and works to empower entrepreneurs in less privileged countries in partnership with the White House, the US State Department, and the United Nations. His model for legacy inspires my own.

CHARITY VERSUS LEGACY

Ever since I was little, I've always "done charity." I started fundraising when I was in primary school. I was the kid who did the 40-hour famine every year. I was the student council president and then, after I left school, I competed in the Miss Australia pageant. I won the title of Miss Fundraiser for my area.

To be honest, that's when I first started to realize that I was really good at making money. Until then I wasn't really interested in being a business owner. My role models weren't business owners. I always thought I'd work for somebody else. But when I made good money for Miss Australia I thought, *oh, I'm actually good at this. I could do this for a business.*

So I did go into business, and I did make money. Figuring out the best way to give some of that money away was just a matter of coming full circle.

But I didn't figure out how to make my giving really effective until I thought about entrenching it in my business. I'd always donated to charity, but there was nothing intentional about it. I wasn't building anything.

That's the difference between doing charity and creating a legacy. Your legacy is something that you live every day. It's something you're building, that will last after you're gone. It's not just about money; it's about giving your time and effort to things that matter, being habitually generous in all circumstances (even when your financial resources are limited), and being a living example to people around you.

Contributing to charity is a great way to give back. But creating a legacy is about so much more than making donations.

Effective Generosity: Why You Shouldn't Start a Charity

Let's say you *do* have the capacity for financial generosity. You're very successful and you want to give back. There's that one cause you're really passionate about and you're determined make a difference. You should start a charity, right?

No, you shouldn't. Starting a charity is a luxury you can grant yourself when you're a billionaire. Otherwise it's a bad idea. Here's why: starting a charity is distracting and very expensive. You'll find your attention taken up with trying to raise money for your own charity when you could just be giving to an existing one. There are 1.6 billion charities in the United States alone, and countless more around the world. Why not support one of those?

(Continued)

> *(Continued)*
>
> It doesn't make sense to put energy into a new charity when there are already so many operating. The best thing you can do is to outsource your effort by supporting an existing charity. Then use your time to make more money, and be more generous.
>
> If you want to start a charity because you've got a pet project or because you want your own name on it, you might need to take a good hard look at your motivations!

LEGACY THROUGH BUSINESS

Entrepreneurship isn't the destination, it's a tool. If you want to make the world a better place, unleash an army of entrepreneurs.

—Jeff Hoffman

We talk about legacy a lot in Entrepreneur's Organization. I used to hear that and think, I'm a marketer. What could I possibly do to change the world? But now I'm a firm believer that business is going to change the world.

Billionaires won't fix the world's problems—although lots of wealthy people are doing an amazing job, there's just not enough of them, and we have to hope that each one becomes a philanthropist. Relying on super-rich people to throw large donations at the problems isn't going to fix everything.

And we can't expect the government alone to change the world. They are slow to move and really only have a true impact when it comes to policies and refuge. Small to medium businesses represent 70% of the US economy. Those businesses are where the real potential for change lies. Imagine if every one of them incorporated giving back into their business model—how much difference could that make?

There are different ways to make giving part of how you do business. I personally believe that the Buy1Give1 model[1] (better known now as B1G1) is a great initiative—so much so that I only invest in businesses that agree to structure it into their business model, if they're not doing it already.

In the B1G1 model, giving is triggered by small, regular actions that your business does. Every time you earn something, you give something back. For example, when you make an online sale, a tree is planted. Or each time you onboard a new client, they can choose whether to buy a goat for a family in Africa or pay a child's school fees for a year.

All the B1G1 partner projects are in line with the UN's Sustainable Development Goals. And your impacts are automatically tracked, so you can watch how quickly your contribution grows.

> The reason that Tamara's businesses work is because she does certain things habitually in those businesses. In the same way, when you give habitually, amazing things happen.
>
> —Paul Dunn, Chairman of Buy1Give1

The Sustainable Development Goals: A global reason to give back

In September 2015, the United Nations agreed to adopt 17 Sustainable Development Goals, also known as the Global Goals.[2] They're a list of ambitious targets to hit by 2030.

The list represents goals for poverty and hunger; health; sanitation; education; environmental sustainability; equality, peace, and justice; economic growth; and innovation.

The incredible thing about these goals is that none of them rely on governments signing on to make them happen. In fact, as Unilever CEO Paul Polman said:, "The SDGs can't be solved without business. It has to mainly be done by the private sector."[3] If these goals are going be achieved, it'll be entrepreneurs and business people that do it.

You might be reading this and thinking one or both of these things:

Entrepreneurs are going to change the world—good for them, but that's not me! I'm not the kind of person who starts multimillion-dollar businesses. How am I supposed to make a difference?

This "legacy" thing is great for rich people, but I'm not there yet! I'll start giving back when I start making real money.

Legacy isn't just about money. And you don't have to do it through business, like I do. Legacy is about giving yourself to what matters. It's about deciding what you want people to say at your funeral, then living a life that creates that lasting impression.

You can do it no matter what circumstances you're in, what vocation you have, or how much capacity you have to give.

And you can start right now. No excuses.

> You don't need profit to give back. Don't make that your excuse. Time and talent are things you have to give that are very valuable to people. Don't say "when I get rich I'll give back" ... You can always do something that matters.
>
> —Jeff Hoffman

LEGACY FOR YOUR LOVED ONES

> The goal is to plant seeds for trees that will bear fruit long after you're gone. You're probably not going to be around to see the true impact of your legacy, and that's okay. Your kids—all they really want is connection. When you're gone someday they don't want the money, they don't want the business, they want connection. How are you going to be able to connect with your kids after you're gone?
>
> —Michel Kripalani, entrepreneur and creator of the Mindset for Success app

We all want to provide something for our family to inherit after we're gone. But you can leave a legacy that's worth so much more than money.

Think about this: When you're gone, would you rather leave your kids with a big inheritance or a big impact? Would you rather they've got your money or memories of you? Would you prefer to build them an investment portfolio or invest in teaching them to live full lives that make an impact?

I'm not saying you can't do both. Just don't focus on the short-term goal of trying to accumulate an inheritance to leave behind and lose sight of the long-term impact you can make on your loved ones that will carry on even after your time on earth is over.

Michel Kripalani, an app developer, created a daily coaching app that delivers motivational messages every morning. I've heard him talk about the moment he realized that his daughters would be able to receive coaching from him for the rest of their lives, even if he was hit by a bus tomorrow.

Another entrepreneur created an email account for each of his children when they were born. If anything happens to him and his wife, their kids will have access to years' worth of emails that their parents have been sending to mark significant moments in their lives.

Jeff Hoffman tells the story of his best friend Michael, who died in an accident when he was in his thirties. Michael wasn't successful by any traditional definition—he had no fame, money, or power—but he loved every second of his life. After Michael's death, Jeff came up with a new definition of a successful person:

"Any person who can stop at that moment in their life, turn around, look back on their life and say, 'What a ride. I've used my time on Earth well. I would not change a thing.'"

Isn't that the example you'd like to leave for your loved ones? Isn't that the type of life you'd like to lead? A life lived so that your loved ones will think of you and say, "She used her life well."

LEGACY BY LIVING EXAMPLE

People are always watching you. Your friends, your employees, and especially your kids. Your life is an example to other people, whether you intend it to be or not. So make sure the life you're living reflects the kind of example that you want to be.

I want to live a life that inspires other people. That might sound like a big call, but an inspiring life doesn't have to be extraordinary. I don't think I'm special. Everybody's got something unique to add—something you bring to the conversation that nobody else is saying. Live a life that you'd be proud for people to copy.

You can create a legacy just by sharing your story. This book is part of my legacy. It might not end poverty or save the world, but maybe I can change the conversation around women, work, and "balance." By talking about the way I shape my life to honor my values, I want to give other people permission to live their own version of a value-centered life. The conversation will get a little bit bigger. More voices will be added. And more women will make choices that have a ripple effect for good.

Your life has incredible power—it's a living example to everyone who comes into contact with you. What legacy can you live out?

LEGACY GIVES YOU LASER FOCUS

When you get crystal clear on the type of legacy you want to create, everything else fades into the background.

It's like when you become a parent, and suddenly you have a new sense of priorities. So many things you worried about before seem unimportant now. You gain a new level of efficiency because you don't have time to spare. And you choose more effective actions, because you don't want to waste energy on unimportant shit.

Or when you have a health scare and realize that you won't be around forever. You stop putting off that travel you've always wanted to do. You take time off work to spend with your family. All of a sudden you know what really matters in life, and you're not bothered about all the different things demanding your attention. You know where to put your focus, and all the rest is noise.

Getting clear on your legacy is like that. When you know your "why," the type of legacy you want to build, anything that isn't related becomes less important. It's easier to cut out the things that don't contribute and put your time, energy, and money into being the kind of person you want to be. You know what you need to do to make the contribution you're determined to make before you leave this earth.

This is why blending is so important. It's not just a self-indulgent thing. It's a set of skills that helps you maximize what you get out of life so that you can give the most to what really matters. It helps you cut out the crap and make the biggest, best contribution that you can with the resources you've got.

This laser focus opens up your life in unexpected ways. Understanding what I value when it comes to legacy has given me bravery in business. It's helped me walk away from an investor who decided to stop doing Buy1Give1 due to the reduction in his profits. It's helped me reduce the clutter when I'm choosing which businesses to invest in. Most surprisingly, it's given me a unique proposition over other investors when it comes to businesses choosing who they want to go with as a partner.

After all, purpose is a driver for humans. When you have a clear sense of purpose, other people want to work with you. They see your passion and they want to partner with you to impact lives together. My personal thing is that I want to impact 50 million lives a year. When I tell people that I want to have enough businesses to impact 50 million lives, they want to get onboard with me to make it happen.

I love this prompt from Jeff Hoffman to help you drive your legacy. He says:

Imagine that today is your funeral; what would people say about you?' Then write down the answers to these questions:

1. What would people say?
2. What do I wish they would say?
3. What am I actually doing with my life to make that happen? What do I need to do?

Then go and do it.

START NOW

"How many billionaires would it take to fix the world's problems?"

I was on Necker Island with Richard Branson, having a discussion with 30 entrepreneurs from around the world, when somebody asked this question.

Okay, it's great that there *are* billionaires in the world who can make a difference. In Silicon Valley, more people are becoming billionaires faster. Many of them are very much into giving. But I wondered, why is it being left to the select few? Why are we having a conversation about billionaires?

Why do we assume that generosity should be left to the extremely wealthy? Why are we waiting until we're very profitable before we start giving back?

I've been guilty of this. Sure, I've always given to charity, but not consistently. I'd give when the company was profitable, or at Christmastime. "Special occasion charity," I call it.

A lot of us do this—we have bursts of generosity when a big payment comes in, or when our business has a great month. Or we tell ourselves, "I'm working on building up my financial security first. One day when I'm making a lot of money, that'll be my time to give back."

The problem with saying you'll give "one day" when you feel rich enough to afford it is that one day might never come. You'll keep putting it off and putting it off, waiting until you're a little bit wealthier, when you could have been giving a small amount consistently all along.

That's why, if you have a business, I encourage you to entrench giving as a cost of goods, rather than waiting until you're profitable to donate.

The same applies to your personal finances or other resources. Don't wait until you're making a lot of money, or you have a lot of spare time on your hands, to start thinking about giving to others. That day might never come! When will you ever feel like you have enough money or enough energy to be generous, if not now?

Entrench generosity into your life as a cost of living. You can implement the Buy1Give1 model into your personal spending, no matter how much or little you have to share. There are apps you can use to set up "giving triggers" in your daily life—for example, every time you buy a coffee you could automatically donate 10 cents to a clean water project. Or when you complete a five-mile run, you trigger the donation of a vaccine to a child in a developing country. How amazing that would be!

A wonderful family activity is when you dine out together, at the end of the meal when you pay the bill, the kids can feed a less fortunate family for a night via an app. Giving is a learned skill, so teaching your kids the act of small, ongoing giving is a great trait for them to have ingrained.

Small, consistent acts of generosity will probably add up to more overall than random grand gestures. More than that, continuous acts of giving will open you up to more connections and more opportunities to grow your legacy. Make giving a part of your everyday life and you'll cultivate a mindset of generosity. Who knows where it will lead?

The time to start is today. Building a legacy is a little bit like building a snowball. It takes time to get it packed together, but eventually you want to get that snowball rolling. How big do you want to get that snowball? Think about people that have really big legacies—how long have they been doing it?
—Michel Kripalani

The sooner you start, the more impact you can have. I'm not talking purely about the dollars you'll donate over the course of your life. I'm talking about the legacy you can build.

It might be a culture you create in your company, or in your family. That type of thing takes years to become deeply rooted and return results in people's lives.

A friend of mine owns an inspiring business called The Helensvale Group. Instead of giving staff bonuses, the team gets to choose a charity to give to through Buy1Give1. Their goals are set around number of impacts, as well as revenue targets.

It might be a life well-lived that becomes an example for others. In 10 years from now, you'll have a decade of life choices to look back on—and even more so in 20 years, and 50. What kind of life do you want to have lived? What kind of example do you want to be? Start making different choices now, and change the course of your life.

I'm pretty proud that I've started thinking about legacy in my early forties. People who are talking about creating legacies through business are usually older, so I feel I have a decade's head start. I feel like I can make more of an impact by starting now. If you're in your twenties or thirties, even better. You might not be in a place to create huge-scale generosity yet, but you can start making small impacts that will continue to grow.

And if you're older, it's never too late. A lot of people use their retirement to volunteer for a cause. Think about how you can maximize that and move from just doing charity to creating a legacy. How can you dedicate the rest of your life to doing something meaningful that people will talk about when you die? How can you connect with loved ones and be well remembered? How can you continue to influence them after you're gone?

I'm not a religious person, but I have a modern adaptation of the *Manual* written by the first-century stoic philosopher Epictetus. It's a book of principles for living. That's like my Bible.

Epictetus doesn't call it legacy. But we're talking about the same thing:

> Now is the time to get serious about living your ideals. Once you have determined the spiritual principles you wish to exemplify, abide by these rules as if they were laws, as if it were indeed sinful to compromise them.

Don't mind if others don't share your convictions. How long can you afford to put off who you really want to be? Your nobler self cannot wait any longer.

Put your principles into practice—now. Stop the excuses and the procrastination. This is your life! You aren't a child anymore. The sooner you set yourself to your spiritual program, the happier you will be. The longer you wait, the more you will be vulnerable to mediocrity and feel filled with shame and regret, because you know you are capable of better.

From this instant on, vow to stop disappointing yourself. Separate yourself from the mob. Decide to be extraordinary and do what you need to do—now.[4]

That's where a blended life can take you.

So go and blend, baby.

Building Your Bucket List: Legacy

A great place to start is with the question we posed earlier in the chapter: If my funeral were today, what would I want people to say about me? And what do I need to do with my life to make that happen?

Examples to get you started:

Build giving into my personal budget.

Donate a day of my professional skills every month to somebody who can't afford to pay.

Help 100 people escape poverty.

Heal my relationship with a family member.

Leave something behind for my children.

Create a business that will keep helping people after I'm gone.

MY BUCKET LIST: THINGS TO DO FOR MY LEGACY

1. _____
2. _____
3. _____
4. _____
5. _____
6. _____
7. _____
8. _____
9. _____
10. _____

NOTES

1. For an overview of the Buy1Give1 model see M. Sato, *Giving Business: Creating the Maximum Impact in a Meaning-Driven World* (Singapore: Buy1Give1, 2016), www.b1g1.com.
2. The Sustainable Development Goals are listed at https://www.un.org/sustainable development/sustainable-development-goals/.
3. M. Mace, "Sustainable Development Goals: Businesses Urged to Take the Lead," *Edie,* September 25, 2015, https://www.edie.net/news/6/Sustainable-Development-Goals-SDGs-business-leadership-Paris-2015/.
4. Epictetus, *A Manual for Living*, a new interpretation by Sharon Lebell (New York: HarperOne, 1994).

PART

Keep Blending for Life

CHAPTER **18**

Things to Do Because I Want To

Build your own blended life

This is a quick guide for how to use the ideas in this book. You can use the steps to map your own version of a blended life that delivers on the things you value most.

This isn't a miracle method, a program, or a set of rules. It's just a way to help you identify the things *you* value, list the areas of life *you* need to manage, and implement *your* unique opportunities for blending.

Just think of it as a way to write a to-do list of things you actually want to do.

THINGS TO DO BECAUSE I WANT TO: A STEP-BY-STEP GUIDE

1. Values Audit

Identify your values first, so that you know what to ditch and where to focus. Then you can make blending choices that will create a life that's aligned with what you value most.

Reference: Chapter 5
Exercise: "Values Audit"

2. Values Hierarchy

Now you know what you want—but the reality is, you can't always have everything you want, all the time.

Prioritizing your values gives you a more sophisticated understanding of how to manage your time and energy without getting burnt out.

I won't say you'll *never* feel guilt or regret when you have to choose one thing or another. Life isn't perfect and sometimes it's hard to get this right.

But you're much more likely to make decisions and come to a resolution faster. This beats the old method of wasting time deliberating and listening to unproductive voices bounce around in your head. Secondly, you'll start to love your decisions and feel okay with "missing out," because you'll know that you put the most important things first.

Reference: Chapter 5

Exercise: "Values Hierarchy"

3. Areas of Life

In this book, I've divided my life up into several areas.

Self	Self-care
	Growth
Work	Career
	Finances
Personal	Marriage
	Parenting
	Friends and Community
	Social Contribution and Legacy

Use mine if they're perfect for you, or come up with a version that suits your own reality.

Make a list that covers all the areas of life that demand your attention—and that you want to give attention to.

Whatever your picture of fulfillment looks like.

4. Aligning Your Life with Your Values

Across every area of life, ask yourself:

How am I honoring my values in this area?

How am I *not* honoring my values in this area?

Which values are most important to me in this area and what am I happy to let slide?

What would it look like to live in alignment with my values in this area?

What specific changes do I need to make to get there?

5. Blending Opportunities

Now that you're starting to get a picture of what you want your life to look like, look for overlap between the different areas of life. Where can you see opportunities to blend?

What kinds of activities light up multiple values at once? What kinds of activities help you fulfil your commitments and desires across multiple areas of life at once?

6. Blending Conversations

Blending is not a solo activity—the way you run your life obviously impacts people around you. Once you've identified some ways to blend, invite other people to try it with you.

You will probably also need to say no to some things that you've decided aren't worth your time and energy or that don't contribute to the blend. You'll need to make changes in some relationships moving forward.

Write a list of the conversations you'll need to have to make the blend happen.

Reference: Chapter 11

Exercise: "Making Agreements" in Chapter 13

7. Write Your Bucket List

Throughout the book, there are opportunities to stop and brainstorm some ideas for your bucket list.

If you've already done that, go back through the chapters and use those ideas as the basis for your list. 100 items is my magic number, but you can have as many or as few as you like—better to have 15 items that make you feel alive than 100 things that don't feel exciting or true to yourself.

Go wild with your bucket list. This is a list of dreams, not an exam you have to pass. Feel free to use your imagination and dream as big as you like. Check out our social for inspiration from others on their lists. Have fun!

Reference: Chapter 7

Exercise: "Building Your Bucket List" boxes in Chapters 7–17

8. Set Goals

Your bucket list is a great place to start when it comes to identifying your immediate goals. For example, if your bucket list says "Live in a foreign country for a year," there will be steps and goals involved to make that happen—a financial goal, a language to learn, a career opportunity to pursue. Each of those can become a shorter-term goal that contributes to the dream on your bucket list.

Remember, writing them down increases the chances of them happening by 70%!

You'll also have other goals that aren't necessarily bucket list items, but are still important to you. Identify the goals you need to achieve to have the life you want to have.

Remember that goals change. It's not always about the goal; it's about the action that you're going to take to get towards that goal that's going to set you off in the direction you want your life to go. Your goals will evolve as you keep growing.

Reference: Chapter 6

Exercise: "Goal-Setting Formula" in Chapter 6

Conclusion

WHAT'S NEXT?

Abolishing Balance Together

Now what?

You've read the book, but I don't want it to end here for you.

Saying no to balance and yes to blending isn't just about creating personal fulfillment for yourself (although I truly hope it brings you that). It's about saying no and yes for women (and men) everywhere—anyone who's stuck in a life they didn't create, serving other people's agendas. I honestly believe that blending can change the world.

The bullying and harassment of women isn't going away. I think it needs to die out, but in the meantime we need to create a much bigger tribe. Together we can stamp out unacceptable and unethical behavior that impacts women and men. I'm not just talking about tangible harassment; I'm talking about corporate power plays, unhealthy competition, and the culture that says we need to keep climbing the ladder at the expense of our health and families.

Some people will be happy to keep you boxed in, serving them. They'll come out fighting against blending. But we need to take care of ourselves first.

Leave any situation that brings you down. Leave any situation where the people in power don't appreciate that blending is the most productive way to work and the best way to build culture. Leave any situation where your superiors or colleagues seek control and alienate you.

I've had experiences that would make most people quit, but we must change the model. For the self-employed, change will come easier. If you are employed, you might need to make bolder moves if your employee doesn't agree and wants control. And for the businesses that want to explore blending in their workplace, let's start the conversation.

You are not alone. You have our support.

At Loehrblend we welcome honest, no ego, no B.S. sharing of what's working and what's not. Let's support each other to achieve the life we want based on each of our unique values. Absolutely no judgment.

This is a global, virtual movement. Join one of our online courses to work through the blending exercises in a group, and find support from the community while you transition into the life you've designed.

For more information visit www.loehrblend.com.

Have the courage to think big and play big and boldly share this with others. Let me go first. Here is my dream: I started a new business called the Dollar Beauty Tribe. It's a solution for all women who have paid money and bought products they've been disappointed with. Instead, I've reversed the model. We allow you to try products (a full sized product – not just a sample) before you buy them. I curate the best of the best products that relate to skincare, haircare, nutrition and wellness, ensuring they are ALL Vegan, Cruelty-Free and Ethical.

Why? Because together we have the purchasing power to abolish animal testing, demand high-efficacy products and positively impact the world via our Buy1Give1 commitment with every product sold. Imagine the impact we could collectively make by changing our beauty buying behaviours.

To join our tribe visit www.dollarbeautytribe.com.

Lastly, if you got value from this book, we invite you to pay it forward to someone you believe would also get value. Think of anyone you know who is a perfect fit for our Work-Life Blenders community, and buy them a copy. Every time you do, we'll donate to Buy1Give1 to provide a business loans to women in developing countries.

This isn't a book you read, get inspired and put away. If you want to take action it's going to take time, and you need support. Let's abolish the word Balance together and become Work-Life Blenders.

Index of Coaching Exercises

Topic/Section	Exercise	Chapter
Foundations		
Values	Values Audit	Chapter 5
	Values Hierarchy	
Goals	What Are My Motivations?	Chapter 6
	Goal-Setting Formula	
Self		
Spiritual	What Do I Belong To?	Chapter 8
Physical	Find Your Physical Thing	Chapter 8
Emotional	Dealing with Emotions	Chapter 8
Intellectual	Write a List of Curiosities	Chapter 9
Work		
Finances	Breaking Through Beliefs	Chapter 12
	Money Mindset Reconditioning	Chapter 12
Personal		
Marriage and Romance	Making Agreements	Chapter 13
Family and Parenting	Create a Family Framework	Chapter 14
	Who Do You Want to Be?	Chapter 14
	Presence Listening	Chapter 15
Friends and Community	Go on an Acquaintance Diet	Chapter 16

Index